THE BIRD LO

THE

Bird Lovers

by

Jens Bjørneboe

Translated from the Norwegian and with an Introduction by Frederick Wasser

LOS ANGELES
SUN & MOON PRESS
1994

Sun & Moon Press
A Program of The Contemporary Arts Educational Project, Inc.
a nonprofit corporation
6026 Wilshire Boulevard, Los Angeles, California 90036

This edition first published in paperback in 1994 by Sun & Moon Press
10 9 8 7 6 5 4 3 2 1
FIRST ENGLISH LANGUAGE EDITION

Orignially published as *Fugleelskerne*
by Gyldendal Norsk Forlag, Oslo, Norway
Published by agreement with Gyldendal Norsk Forlag

This book was made possible, in part, through an operational grant from the Andrew W. Mellon Foundation and through contributions to The Contemporary Arts Educational Project, Inc., a nonprofit corporation

Cover: Susan Bee, *Flight of the Albatross*
Collection of Peter Straub

LIBRARY OF CONGRESS CATALOGING IN PUBLICATION DATA
Bjørneboe, Jens (1920-1976)
The Bird Lovers (Fugleelskerne)
p. cm — (Sun & Moon Classics: 43)
ISBN: 1-55713-146-5
I. Title. II. Series.
811'.54—dc20

Printed in the United States of America on acid-free paper.

TRANSLATOR'S INTRODUCTION

Jens Bjørneboe has been firmly established as a preeminent novelist and dramatist of postwar Europe. Despite this he has yet to be adequately introduced to the American scene. This translation of "Fugleelskerne" (*The Bird Lovers*) is the first time his theatrical work has been presented to the English speaking world. This pioneering Sun and Moon edition should lead to a long deserved reappraisal.

Therefore my introduction will be a plea, an advocacy of the importance of Bjørneboe's writings as we approach the twentieth anniversary of his premature death in 1976. Unfortunately, the central problem of his work has only increased in importance since his death. The tragicomic plotline of *The Bird Lovers* continues to be played out over and over again from Argentina to El Salvador, from Cambodia to the former East Germany and on into the near future of South Africa and the former Yugoslavia. The problem is simple to state; what price does Justice demand for crimes committed in the name of the State? The answer is impossible to know (as the Hunting Club of Torre Rosse will find out in the second act). How does the demand of Justice for retribution differ from personal vengeance (reserved for the Divine in the Old Testament)? Or can Justice forgive the agents of an evil State, an option that as far back as *Antigone* has smacked of complacency?

The hunters of a small Italian town are being pressured by German tourists to stop shooting song birds. In the course of their negotiations, they recognize two of the Germans as former military officers. These officers conducted tortures, punishments and executions two decades previously when the Nazis controlled this part of Italy. The Italians capture them and conduct a kangaroo trial as the preliminary to hanging them. But the Germans appeal to their sense of justice and succeed in getting the local defrocked priest to plea for them.

Father Piccolino tries every moral argument he can think of to get his fellow townsmen to understand the problem of moral agency in the actions individuals commit during a war. In these arguments Bjørneboe catalogs the legacy of evil that is the history of all civilizations. But the Italians are buying none of this. The Germans must die! Until Piccolino introduces one more consideration; a consideration that he argues not as an abstract moralizer but as a priest, as someone trying desperately to save two men from death. It is the consideration of economic self improvement: greed.

The play now takes its comic bitter trajectory towards its final dénouement as the Italians realize, one by one, which side of their bread is buttered. The final burlesque of the crucifixion provides an electrifying ending that dissolves ironically into Beethoven's Ninth Symphony.

Though Bjørneboe's vision is unrelentingly dark, his commitment to the values of the theater engages the audience in an exciting participation. He delights in irony and often takes a grim joy in ambiguity. His theater is high energy with songs ranging from romantic to brutal, colorful staging and cross-cutting the humorous with the grotesque. His self acknowledged mentor is Bertolt Brecht but the juicy quality of *The Bird Lovers* avoids the analytic dryness of the alienation techniques (Verfremdung) that Brecht uses.

Jens Bjørneboe had a certain humility towards writing for the theater since his dramatic work represents a fraction of his prose writings. Therefore he felt very strongly that he had to learn from the theater and remain true to the demands of drama rather than to dictate and to insist on the same values he had in his novels. Therefore though *The Bird Lovers* contains similar arguments and themes as the novels, it is a totally different type of work.

In all his work, Bjørneboe is cataloging evil. The overwhelming legacy of evil is the central theme of the autobiographical memories, visions and musings that make up the trilogy of novels he unified under the heading *The History of Bestiality*; "Frihetens øyeblikk" (translated in English as *Moment of Freedom*), "Kruttårnet" and "Stillheten."

This occupation was determined by his own place in history. He was twenty years old when the Germans conquered Norway in the early part of World War Two.

Bjørneboe did not participate in that fighting though he did try to join a unit in the chaos of the invasion. He remained in the country until the Nazis began calling up able bodied Norwegians to serve in their armies. Bjørneboe walked across the border into neutral Sweden and spent the rest of the war there studying painting.

After the war the young man became obsessed with the enormity of Nazi crimes. German was a second language for his family, who were in the import/export business. He felt it was part of his culture and his moral responsibility. He travelled throughout Germany and Europe after the war, sending reports back to Norwegian newspapers. His first novel was a story of the doctors who had conducted the inhuman practices of the death camps. It drew the acclaim of Norwegian society.

But Bjørneboe did not settle for the easy condemnation that other Norwegians could use to repudiate the Nazi regime. In his next novel he explored the hypocrisies of the way, after the war, Norway treated her own citizens who had collaborated with the occupying forces. This second novel created a fierce controversy and established Bjørneboe as the moral gadfly of Norway, a position he never gave up. He wrote countless newspaper polemics and was sued and issued counter-suits during the active part of his career. He was convicted in 1967 of writing a pornographic novel *Without a Stitch* ("Uten en tråd") in a famous trial. He went on to write about local miscarriages of justice, politics, education, the brutality of the prison system, the Vietnam war, and sexual hypocrisy.

He returned to these matters because he could not find the line that absolves any member of society for the evil actions of that society. His purpose is to confront us with our own evil, to remind us constantly that it takes only a dark wind to deprive quiet stable men of all restraint and to drive them to butcher their servants, wives and daughters. Yet in all his writings, Bjørneboe cannot find a solid moral basis for judgment. We are strangely deprived of any cathartic release from the catalog of immorality we are confronted with. Neither God nor Lucifer can secure our moral values. The central character of *Moment of Freedom* can catalog evil but cannot absolve himself of it except through the amnesia of alcohol and travel. John Hoberman (1976) and Joe Martin (1987) have expressed surprise at the lack of a moral system. "For an author so preoccupied with atrocity, Bjørneboe has remarkably little sense of sin in the personal sense...This author will send mankind to the confessional, but he will not confess" (Hoberman, 67). It is perhaps in this inability to draw a moral line that Bjørneboe moves beyond the great Norwegian moralists of the nineteenth century such as Ibsen who could still maintain notions of individual responsibility. Bjørneboe writes for morally aware members of societies where an abstract and omnipresent Authority is in control. Only an uncompromising commitment to total rebellion can hope to establish a place separate from this Authority. But anyone who has tried this path knows its heavy human toll, a toll that contributed to Bjørneboe's own self-destruction.

This dilemma can be reframed in a postmodern concern with the lack of grand narrative, the multi-vocal discourse of many local narratives. However the human problem is that the grand narrative of evil is still as powerful as ever, while the local narratives of responsibility cannot control effective action. The position of a Norwegian is exemplary of this trap. The idea of Norway was innocently implicated by the race myths of the Nazis. In their ideology Norway represented the ideal of a Germanic "Volk" community with hardly any impure elements mixed in. The Nazis not only celebrated the purity of the Norwegians but also their rustic lifestyle and attachments. This fitted in all too well with their own slogan of "blood and earth." Thus Norway found itself coopted into a Nazi vision despite the overwhelming opposition of Norwegians to such homegrown fascists as Quisling and to the German occupation.

Therefore this official history of resistance with which Norway prides itself did not satisfy Bjørneboe. He could not be sure of his own righteousness nor that of his country. His writing returns over and over again to the shortcomings of his society be it Norway, Northern Europe or Western Civilization. Local claims of absolution are not good enough for this universal problem of civilization. Indeed Janet Garton reports that he objected to the first staging of this play as too specific in its references to Germany (Garton 78). He wanted the audience to understand the problems as universal, particularly in the world after the dropping of the atomic bomb.

In the play he allows Italians a way out of their desire for revenge. They refrain from killing the two men because of their identities as would-be capitalists. Though this motivation saves them it does not do them honor.

The group may be justified in their primary concern with survival but this is only a provisional answer that closes off the staged drama.

But the individual has to find something deeper, something that preserves both honor and survival. Caruso is the last hold out because he wants the *individual* satisfaction of justice. He is the one character who is always the last to join the group, the first to stand out. His entrance is announced in a unique manner. He is the only character who is depicted at home. The whole focus of the group is upon him as the leader and it is from this position that he tries to hold out for justice. This is the final realization of his sin, that he is holding out for a justice that will destroy the group and for this he seeks forgiveness from the ultimate practitioners of groupthink; "the Good Germans." It is especially significant that his final act of contrition is not to the Judge but to Johannes, the subordinate.

Bjørneboe never displayed any interest in the group in his novels. The Court's servant in *Moment of Freedom* is all alone in his confrontation with the bestiality of the world and in his solitariness he can find no answer. For him, for the individual suffering from association with the guilt of the collective, the only response left is laughter. Perhaps this is a reason that he was drawn to the Italian setting. Here is a country which has taught itself to laugh after having endured two millennia of being the plaything of every passing tyrant. In his novel, he tells the story of the Renaissance satirist, Pietro Aretino's laughing himself to death when he finds his sister in a bordello (*Moment of Freedom* p. 112). The laughter dissolves its own hypocrisy, and so Bjørneboe came to love Italy as he could not forgive the smugness of the Northern European morality, ignoring its own evil lapses from prim virtue.

Laughter can actually be heard in the theater and so Bjørneboe goes from merely speculating on it in the novel to actually being funny on the stage. *The Bird Lovers* can laugh at the horror that has distorted the moral conscious of this century. The grotesque oppositions are funny, even between cooking and execution, one laughs because there's no point in crying. Even the German Judge allows himself a smile. And so we can only hope to exit laughing.

My own encounter with his work occurred when I was sitting in a nightclub in Bergen with several of my younger Norwegian friends, three months after the Berlin Wall had been opened. I challenged them for their favorite author and the answer was immediate; Jens Bjørneboe, a man of whom I had never heard. I purchased his books the next day and started to read them in the soft drizzle of a Norwegian spring and soon realized how much he spoke to the heart of our responsibility as members of a society where evil and power are so intertwined as to leave no one untouched, leaving all both victim and guilty of victimizing.

Norwegian may be a small language but is a large one in world literature. In consultation with Douglas Messerli, I have tried to make this a literary translation and hope that the emphatic nature of the original can still be heard in the English. Bjørneboe wrote directly in both his novels and plays. There is an inherent rhythm to the Norwegian line that would have sounded mannered if reproduced into English. I have made no attempt to restore the rhymes of the lyrics. Bjørneboe had no concern with the political struggles for restoring the purity of the Norwegian language and used the urban variant now known as "bokmål." This reflected his internationalist outlook.

I especially wish to acknowledge my mother, Solidelle Fortier Wasser, who not only does all the good things that mothers do for their literary children who so often acknowledge them in their publications but who also was extraordinarily generous with her gift of languages on this project and patiently corrected my drafts several times. I also wish to thank Arve Øverland for his original tip about Bjørneboe and Epsen Aarseth for the many conversations we have had about Bjørneboe and other aspects of contemporary literature. Despite the best efforts of my Norwegian friends I am sure there are infelicities that only I can take responsibility for.

Frederick Wasser
1993, Champaign, Illinois

BJØRNEBOE IN ENGLISH OUT OF PRINT

The Least of These (translated from "Jonas") Indianapolis: Bobbs-Merill, 1959.

Without a Stitch (translated from "Uten en tråd") New York: Grove Press, 1969

Moment of Freedom. (translated from "Frihetens øyeblikk") New York: Norton, 1975.

"The Powder Magazine" (an excerpt from "Kruttårnet") *Prism International* . University of British Columbia. Winter 1980 vol. 19 no. 2:32-39.

ANNOUNCED FOR JUNE 1993

The Sharks: The History of a Crew and a Shipwreck (translated from "Haiene") Great Britain: Norvik Press.

WORKS ABOUT BJØRNEBOE IN ENGLISH

Garton, Janet. *Jens Bjørneboe: Prophet Without Honor.* Westport: Greenwood, 1985.

Hoberman, John "The Political Imagination of Jens Bjørneboe; A Study of 'Under en hårdere himmel'." *Scandinavian Studies.* Winter 1976: 52 - 70.

Martin, Joseph. *Keeper of the Protocols: The Works of Jens Bjørneboe in the Crossroads of Western Literature.* Ph.D. disseration. University of British Columbia, 1987.

Aarnes, Sigurd. "The Problem of Evil: Nazism in Jens Bjørneboe's Writing." trans. J. Weinstock. in *The Nordic Mind.* eds. Frank Andersen & John Weinstock. New York: University Press of America.

One must remember that man's history, according to Jewish and Greek myths, begins with an act of disobedience. Disobedience is the first free act. Mankind has continued to develop itself through acts of disobedience; our intellectual development is also dependent on the ability to show disobedience.

—ERICH FROMM

PART I

Cast:

HULDREICH VON UND ZU GREIFENKLAU, JUDGE
MRS. DIRECTOR STAHLMANN
MISS HERZ
JOHANNES SCHULZE, SINGING TEACHER
RAFAELE OMBRIOSO, HOTEL OWNER
FIDELE, HOST
PICCOLINO MICHELANGELO, PRIEST
CAVALLI, BARBER
CARUSO, MECHANIC
ROSA, HIS WIFE
SANDRO, FARM WORKER
MARCO, TAXI DRIVER
A POLISH MAN
SOLDIERS

Place: A town by the Mediterranean Sea

Intermission between scenes 23 and 24

Motto: Quäle nie ein Tier zum Scherz,
denn es kann geladen sein.*

(This play premiered in 1966 at the National Theater, Oslo, Norway)

*Bjørneboe's playful mixing of two German proverbs. It means "Do not torture an animal in fun, the creature might be loaded."

■ SCENE I

The bar in Circolo Recreativo; PICCOLINO, FIDELE, CAVALLI, MARCO, *and* SANDRO. *A radio. On the wall the hunting club's emblem.* FIDELE *is listening intently to the radio that cannot be heard.* PICCOLINO *is cleaning the shotgun. The others are drinking wine in silence. Prolonged silence. The scene is in silence as long as possible.*

SANDRO: I like fat women.

Everyone turns to him.

ALL: Ssshh!!

Absolute silence.

FIDELE *turns the radio up loud.*

RADIO VOICE: From Schweinsruhe we have the announcement that the National Society for Animal's Rights has resolved to establish its vacation sanctuary for bird lovers in the Torre Rosse district on the condition that all hunting of songbirds in the area be stopped. The vacation sanctuary is thought to be of the greatest economic importance for the community. If the killing of songbirds is not totally forbidden the Society will A: move its vacation sanctuary to another town B: introduce a total tourist boycott of the whole area.

From Moscow the announcement of the new space ship Ivan the Terrible is now on the way to the planet Jupiter...

All are shouting and stomping.

FIDELE *turns off the radio.*

MARCO: I'll never stop hunting!

CAVALLI: You must. All the money that the vacation packages will bring in...

MARCO: You are a barber.

CAVALLI: You drive a cab.

SANDRO: It is the one and only satisfaction us small timers have.

CAVALLI: Torre Rosse will become a rich town.

SANDRO: I will not stop shooting birds.

Shrieks, stomps, makes violent noises

FIDELE: Sssh. Think about…

MARCO: Wait until Caruso comes.

CAVALLI: He is also poor. We need the money and….

Noise

FIDELE: What do you say Father Piccolino? Is it right to say no thanks?

PICCOLINO: [*Cleaning the shotgun, aims it, etc.*] A sparrow shall not fall to the earth without God knowing it.

CAVALLI: [*Sings*]

Here you meet the Torre Rosse
Our quiet little town.
There's not much to go on,
There's no name or renown.

There you see our friend, Fidele,

Our host and restaurateur.
And here you see friendly Marco,
Our all around driver.

There is Sandro, farm hand.
He lives from day to day.
And here our priest Michelangelo,
hunter and guerrilla fighter.

He is expelled from the clergy
and banished from the sacrament
but a priest is a priest as we all know
both now and evermore.

I myself bear the name Cavalli
and I am the town's hair cutter.
And now comes Caruso,
Mechanic and Saboteur;

CARUSO *enters in a heavy duty hunting outfit.*

■ SCENE 2

ALL: [*Turning enthusiastically to him*] Caruso!

CAVALLI: What have you got?

CARUSO *takes some small birds out of his sack.*

He drinks from a glass on the bar, through the following.

FIDELE: Two larks. Three nightingales.

PICCOLINO: Chestnuts, sherry sauce, truffles and cognac. Black olives. Mushrooms.

FIDELE: Garlic for the nightingale. That's how Grandma did it.

MARCO: Sage, bacon, chicken liver and Marsala.

SANDRO: I only said that I like those fat girls. Is there something wrong in that also? What?!!

MARCO: The bird lovers will stop us, Caruso.

CAVALLI: Caruso doesn't like bird lovers. He's biased.

MARCO: It is not everyone who has been executed and afterwards has risen from the dead. That was in the town of Bonzo.

CARUSO: Twenty years ago Father Piccolino raised me from the dead. That is his only miracle.

CAVALLI: Since Caruso was shot he can't stand bird fanciers. He has become a bigot.

CARUSO: [*Eating olives*] I have nothing against particular people or races. For me a white American is as good as a nigger. A German can be as good as a rag peddling Jew. An Englishman just as good as a devil Irishman. A Frenchman can be as good a man as an Algerian. A dago is also a person. Only I just don't like folk who lord it over others. [ROSA *enters, sees him.*] I can't stand anyone who wants to patronize us!

■ SCENE 3

ROSA: Will you come home right now!

CARUSO: My precious.

MARCO: Rosa, let us remember Benjamin and...

ROSA: Home!

PICCOLINO: Let us remember our dead. Those were the days of signs and wonders.

CARUSO: That was a long time ago. What has happened since?

PICCOLINO: We've grown thicker around the waist.

CARUSO: Benjamino and me. He was Rosa's brother. And there is the Pole and the Judge and his bailiff... [*Marching music.*] Benjamino and I stood here. Rosa there! There where the bar is, was the table with judge and the jury.

FIDELE, PICCOLINO, MARCO, *and* SANDRO *take their places as jurors but they leave an opening in the middle for the* JUDGE. CAVALLI *takes* BENJAMINO'S *place.*

CARUSO: The Pole sat there with the bandage wrapped around where his eyes had been. He clearly hadn't been able to stand since his interrogation. [*Marching music grows louder.*] We are missing the Guard and the Judge and his Bailiff....

Deafening Military Music. JOHANNES *as well as the others enter, dragging the* POLE. *The Symbol of the Occupation; a Big Bird of Prey depicted on a banner drops down in back of the* JUDGE'S *chair. The* JUDGE *enters. All rise.* TWO SOLDIERS *lift the* POLE *up.*

■ SCENE 4

THE JUDGE: [*In a glittering well decorated officer's uniform. He has a package in his hand.*] At ease! [*The others sit except* JOHANNES *who is in a Corporal's uniform.*] Johannes! [*He beckons him with his forefinger.*]

JOHANNES: Yes sir! Herr Major.

THE JUDGE: [*Softly*] Has the Corporal noticed the roses by the old town hall? [*Picks two roses out of the package.*]

JOHANNES: Yes sir, Herr Major.

THE JUDGE: Unusually tender fragrant roses. They struck me as uniquely beautiful when I walked past the town hall on my way. Isn't it so?

JOHANNES: Yes sir, Herr Major.

THE JUDGE: The petals are especially lovely, like music. They are beautiful...beautiful. Does the Corporal believe that they can be taken up and planted somewhere else?

JOHANNES: Yes sir, Herr Major.

THE JUDGE: They are sturdy. [JOHANNES *holds the judicial cap for him while the* THE JUDGE *puts it on.*] Yes, the cap, yes. They certainly will stand the Northern climate, eh? [*Puts on his judicial robes*]

The Corporal believes that?

JOHANNES: Yes sir, Herr Major. With care and kindness. They must be loved.

THE JUDGE: Love them. That is the order.

JOHANNES: Thank you, Herr Major.

THE JUDGE: Put these in water.

JOHANNES: Yes sir, Herr Major.

THE JUDGE: Dig up the whole rose bed by the town hall and pack the gathered rose bushes well with mulch and wet newspapers. You will send these to my private quarters. Understood? [*Puts on his* JUDGE's *gloves, long and red like a hangsman's.*]

JOHANNES: Yes sir, Herr Major.

THE JUDGE: Did the Corporal hear the nightingale last night?

JOHANNES: Nightingale, Herr Major.

THE JUDGE: It sang wonderfully like an angel of God in ethereal tones.

JOHANNES: Ethereal tones, Herr Major.

THE JUDGE: [*Takes his seat*] The court is in session.

ROSA: Jesus Maria!

THE JUDGE: [*Gaveling*] Ssssh...

THE POLE: [*Slumping down*] Ahh...a....[*Groping blindly*]

THE JUDGE: Grab him!

TWO SOLDIERS: [*Holding him up*] Yes sir, Herr Major.

THE JUDGE: [*Looks at the papers before him*] The examining officer is Corporal Johannes Schulze, in civilian life a teacher of music and gymnastics.

JOHANNES: Music and gymnastics, Herr Major.

THE JUDGE: As examining Officer you are the chief witness in the case against the four defendants. Number One Caruso Gentile, Number Two Benjamino Verde, Number Three Janusz Swiderski, Number Four Rosa Verde. Is that correct?

JOHANNES: Yes sir, Herr Major.

THE JUDGE: Defendants One, Two and Four have declared themselves guilty of having helped rescue a person—to having received and hidden defendant Number Three who was escaping from the local work camp Rosenhain in the district of Torre Rosse by the town Bonzo. Also defendant Number Three has made a full confession. Is that correct?

JOHANNES: Yes sir, Your Honor. One and all have confessed fully.

ROSA: Jesus Maria! Save us Mother of God.

THE JUDGE: [*Gavelling hard*] Respect for the court! *Respect for the court!*

CARUSO: Your Honor, the confessions were made after a long torture.

Silence

ROSA: Just look at us.

JOHANNES: [*Pulling his glove off and hitting them*] Your Honor! The examination was conducted in exact compliance with the regulations.

THE POLE: [*Falls to the floor and tries to crawl*] Ahh...a...

THE JUDGE: Hold him upright before the court!

SOLDIERS: [*Lifting him up while shaking and hitting him*] Yes sir, Herr Chief Judge. Yes sir Herr Major. Pull yourself together you swine.

ROSA: Jesus Maria, spread your mercy over us.

THE JUDGE: Members of the court having familiarized themselves with the case's documents, will now pronounce their sentence. [*Music*].

JURORS: [*Standing up*] Yes sir Your Honor.

THE JUDGE: [*Sitting*] Defendant number One.

The following as ritual, sung in falling tones

JUROR ONE: Guilty.

JUROR TWO: Guilty.

JUROR THREE: Guilty.

JUROR FOUR: Guilty.

THE JUDGE: Defendant number Two.

JUROR ONE: Guilty.

JUROR TWO: Guilty.

JUROR THREE: Guilty.

JUROR FOUR: Guilty.

THE JUDGE: Defendant number Three.

JUROR ONE: Guilty.

JUROR TWO: Guilty.

JUROR THREE: Guilty.

JUROR FOUR: Guilty.

THE JUDGE: Defendant number Four.

JUROR ONE: Guilty.

JUROR TWO: Guilty.

JUROR THREE: Guilty.

JUROR FOUR: Guilty.

ROSA: Oh Jesus Maria!

THE JUDGE: [*Standing, singing*] In consideration of the

fact that the court's learned and impartial members have thoroughly examined the documents, both for and against, in the case, taking all the evidence in account and holding that all the defendants' own considered statements substantiate the case against them; the court has found the four defendants guilty of all the State's charges; that is to have escaped themselves or to have abetted avoidance and escape from imprisonment. By their actions they have placed the security of Europe at risk.

THE JUDGE and JURORS: [*Chanting*] The sentence of the court;

THE JUDGE: Because of the evil nature of the case, the law's strongest punishment must be applied. Defendant number One—execution by the firing squad. Defendant number Two—execution by the firing squad. Defendant number Three—execution by the firing squad. Defendant number Four—twenty years in the penitentiary. The court's judgment is irrevocable and the sentence will be carried out immediately.

ROSA: [*Shrieking loudly*] Jesus Maria! [*Screaming*] These are my brother and my husband! Maria!

BENJAMINO: Let me go. I don't want to die now.

THE POLE: [*Casts himself on the ground and crawls around blindly*] Oh..

CARUSO: Murderers!

THE JUDGE: Defendant number One merits additional punishment for this outburst. The court is adjourned. [*Crosses to* JOHANNES *who helps him with his cap and gloves*] Shoot them!

JOHANNES: Thank you, Herr Major.

ALL: [*Screams, followed by silence.*]

CARUSO: [*Approaching the proscenium. Sings*]

"Caruso Death Song"

Now the day has arrived and the hour has arrived.
And you are placed against the wall to bleed.
And the ones who hold you dear
Soon fade away from you
That's when you will see; it is lonesome to die.

Before the day has arrived and the hour has arrived.
And the sand you stand on, you have colored red.
When they are taking you to the other side

you'll remember what I said,
Brother it is really lonesome to be dead.

PUNISHMENT: CARUSO *is whipped by* JOHANNES *in the following. It is an abstract pantomine.* CARUSO *crawls on the floor and* JOHANNES *follows with the whip. One hears the beating very clearly.*

THE JUDGE: I have never heard such a nightingale so remarkably beautiful as here…[*Whip crack.*]

JOHANNES: [*Hitting.*] Yes sir Herr Judge.

THE JUDGE: It is as if I was a child and was hearing it for the first time [*Whip crack.*] Those tones of a grand heavenly flute. [*Whip crack.*]

JOHANNES: [*Hitting.*] Yes sir, Your Honor.

THE JUDGE: My God, it is beauty's sacrament. [*Whip crack.*]

JOHANNES: [*Hitting.*] Yes sir, Herr Advocate. The Beauty!

THE JUDGE: And finally, see to it that the roses are packed professionally. [*Whip crack.*] Professionally!

JOHANNES: [*Finished hitting.*] Yes sir, Herr Major. Professionally.

The Court breaks up with shrill military music. Rifle salvoes are heard from the firing squad.

SCENE 5

Circolo Recreativo, the bird emblem and soldiers gone.

CARUSO: Up against the wall and pang. To be shot is the most disgusting thing I know.

MARCO: It is much worse to be hanged. Do you remember how they squirmed?

PICCOLINO: I was the official chaplain at the execution. It was in the late afternoon. It had rained. Caruso was still moving after the shooting. After it became dark I went back and got him. First we hid him in the town, then we went up into the mountains.

FIDELE: When he had recovered, both Caruso and Father Piccolino came to us.

CARUSO: To the partisans!

ALL: To the partisans!

MARCO: When we see the squirming, you must understand that hanging is worse. It goes on the longest.

CAVALLI: The hunting club is composed of the former Partisan group "43".

ROSA: Now you must go home! Right now!

FIDELE: [*To Rosa*] We know that you were left in the penitentiary until the war was over. Will you never stop taking that out on Caruso? [*Plays dance music on the radio.* CARUSO *and* ROSA *dance. They approach the door.*] The hunting bag!

PICCOLINO: See what the day's effort has brought to your husband.

CARUSO: [*Opening the bag*] Rosa!

MARCO: There is the Spanish strangulation; an iron shackle that screws slowly around your neck.

CARUSO: We will have a real dinner today!

CAVALLI: The electric chair is the worst. In America…

ROSA: So delicious.

CAVALLI: In America they also use the gas chamber.

ROSA: ...with white beans.

MARCO: The electric chair isn't so bad. You pass out at once and...

PICCOLINO: Smothered in oil and lemon and garlic. Delicious small birds.

FIDELE: They jump and squirm in the chair for quite a while and it smells like burnt flesh in the room.

PICCOLINO: Do you roast them on a spit, Rosa?

CAVALLI: When the current is on they can't smell it themselves.

CARUSO: It is good panfried also. With oil and butter mixed and sage and a little red wine to top it off.

CAVALLI: But in the gas chamber, there they can smell it as they sit in the chamber and they know the gas is coming.

PICCOLINO: For the sauce you use white wine, Caruso.

SANDRO: ...to be burnt at the stake. There are many who were burnt alive. You remember the military police who rounded up the village people into the church and then poured benzine over the church floor and through the windows. When they ignited it, all those inside were burnt alive in the church. You could hear the burning children screaming from far, far away.

CARUSO: A dry sherry. That is also good.

MARCO: I believe the rack is the worst.

ROSA: White wine is the best.

SANDRO: To be burnt alive at the stake. That is the very worst.

PICCOLINO: To cook them al cacciatore is the very best.

CARUSO: Father Piccolino will sing a song now about the flesh and the spirit.

PICCOLINO: [*Sings*]

"Song of the Flesh and the Spirit"

I gladly eat the bread
I hold in my hand,

for flesh is of the flesh
only the spirit is of the spirit.

I like fat women,
I like chicken breast,
the same with mussels, crawfish and squid,
that come from our coast.

ROSA:

I like morning coffee
that smells strong and fresh.
I like broiled fish
that smells really like fish.

PICCOLINO:

I like roasted doves
and rooster combs and swine.
I like lark's tongues
and song thrush cooked in wine.

ROSA:

I like rugged hunters
who come home from hunting
in the woods full of birds chirping
with their sack full of game.

PICCOLINO:

I like tender larks
and such fine nightingales.

I like thrush heads.
I like cheese and wine.

I gladly eat the bread
I have in my hand.
for flesh is of the flesh
only the spirit is of the spirit.

■ SCENE 6

MISS HERZ *enters. She carries a paste bucket, a brush and a roll of posters.*

HERZ: [*To* CARUSO] Do you kill little birds? A glass of black currant juice, please? [*Silence from the bar*] I will put up a poster here. It will only take a minute.

FIDELE: I am afraid that we don't have black currant juice, Mrs…

HERZ: Miss.

FIDELE: Miss.

HERZ: Yogurt please.

FIDELE: Unfortunately we don't have milk Mrs…

HERZ: Miss. Do you kill little birds? Mineral water.

CAVALLI: Only now and then Miss. He will…

HERZ: …stop doing that, yes. Is it a surprise to you that the delegation from the Bird Lover's Group of the County Society for Animal's Rights is arriving in Torre Rosse.

CARUSO: No but…

HERZ: Nonetheless you continue with the bird killings. [*Concentrating on him, staring him down.*] How are you able to do that!!

FIDELE: [*Serving a glass of mineral water*] Here you go, Miss.

HERZ: A big, strong man should be the animal's protector and friend. Do you eat them?

CARUSO: With onion, tomato and parsley.

HERZ: Haven't you thought about how it must hurt me?

CARUSO: It is not you I eat.

FIDELE: [*Tapping the glass*] Here you go.

HERZ: I can't stand it. The heart...

PICCOLINO: Have a cognac, Miss.

HERZ: [*Stares at him*] Here you sit as a member of the clergy without intervening against bird killing. You even take part occasionally in the hunt against small helpless birds.

SANDRO: He devours several dozen of them without batting an eye.

HERZ: What do you believe St. Francis would have said if he saw you eating Little Sister, the lark. He who treated all animals as our brothers and sisters [*Glares at* CARUSO].

CARUSO: This is a hunting club. Dare I ask what do you wish?

HERZ: [*Ingratiating*] First a promise from all of you; that you will never shoot birds. [*Takes his hand*] After that we'll put up these posters together.

CARUSO: Get lost.

HERZ: [*Clinging to him*] What if I beg you?

CARUSO: Sorry.

HERZ: [*Intimate*] You can't mean that.

MARCO: No posters.

HERZ: Here I come nice and polite and ask you to do this. And yet you refuse. Do you know who the bird lovers are?

PICCOLINO: We can guess.

HERZ: [*Gets a glimpse of Rosa*] Oh I'm in luck, a woman! Certainly you are on my side. Help me with the posters.

ROSA: No.

HERZ: I beg you to do this. It is for the birds' sake. Be so kind. We women must stick together. Don't you think so?

ROSA: No.

HERZ: You won't help me?

PICCOLINO: She stayed too long in jail. It's of no use.

HERZ: God! [*Steps backwards*] In jail. A victim of the fascists.

PICCOLINO: A danger to European security. But she is not as dangerous as she looks. You have to give her the benefit of the doubt.

HERZ: [*Friendly, easy*] Help me with the posters. Be nice.

ROSA: You can go to hell with your posters.

HERZ: What?

ROSA: I am going to take the posters from you and tear them into itty bitty pieces.

HERZ: [*Clinging to Caruso*] Help me!

ROSA: [*Approaching*] You fancy my husband.

CARUSO: There, there, Rosa, control yourself.

ROSA: I only want to peek at her posters.

CARUSO: You are not going to do that.

HERZ: [*Highstrung*] Sure. You're hostile to me. That's not going to be good. But the posters go up.

FIDELE: Let her put up the posters.

MARCO: No.

CAVALLI: She has a right to put up the posters.

ROSA: Not in my lifetime.

HERZ: Don't you know that we shall establish a vacation sanctuary for bird friends here. We are thousands of Bird Lovers.

CAVALLI: That will bring in a lot of money, Rosa, for everyone.

ROSA: [*Thinking about it*] She might as well put up her posters.

SANDRO: No.

HERZ: We have other means then to ask nice and politely. You will *force* us to be hard. Do you want us to use force?

CARUSO: It is our birds who fly here. We hunt them and eat them as much as we want. Moreover I will eat them alive also! The conversation is hereby closed.

HERZ: [*Unrolling the posters on the floor*] Nothing can stop us! Try stopping me from hanging these up! Don't bird lovers have their universal human rights!

SANDRO: No posters.

FIDELE: I'm the one who rents the place. Let her hang them up.

MARCO: No bird posters in our circolo!

FIDELE: Let her hang them up.

CARUSO: It is our hunting club!

CAVALLI: It is obviously a civil right. Please miss, hang them up.

MARCO: Take them away.

HERZ: [*Starts to stir the wheat paste*] It is only a few sheets here. At the most three.

MARCO: Not here. It is our circolo [*Stops her*].

HERZ: [*Crying out*] He's using violence. He's stopping me.

CAVALLI: [*Grabbing him*] Marco. Let her put them up. [*Tries to push* MARCO *who is blocking her.*] Go away. [*They struggle*].

MARCO: [*Pulling free*] Don't you see who is right?

FIDELE: [*Gripping* MARCO] Give it up. You can't solve anything with violence. It is a question of principle. Give it up.

SANDRO: [*Grabs* FIDELE] Stand back. [*All four struggle*]. Come and help us Caruso.

PICCOLINO: [*Getting up*] Stop! She has the law on her side. What's more, she is a lady. Afterwards we'll have the law on our side when we take them down again.

HERZ: You just try! [*She hangs up three posters while the others watch. They are pictures of small birds, who vaguely resemble the emblems of the occupation. They have such text as; "protect our small brothers," "spare the song birds," and "save our small feathered friends!" She packs up her bag and catches* CARUSO *with a glance.*] If you take down our posters we will come back and put up more. We can deck the walls with posters. We can deck the houses with them. We have hundreds, thousands. We have millions of posters. [ROSA *and* CARUSO *exit.*]

Herz to the proscenium and sings

"Fatherland Psalm"

Mercedes' tracks in all the lands.

On all the roads world wide.
Every prosperous businessman,
Mercedes is his pride.

Take Lufthansa for an Easter trip.
Prevent an ulcer and a heart attack
take a trip to Singapore.
All is for sale for a good mark.

A Volkswagen in every home,
in south and north and west.
For a cheap auto in the future,
the people's wagon is always the best.

In Ironworks and Pharmacy
We've become first class,
with Krupps and Bayers Industry
in Crematoriums and Gas.

Our oven is built for quality.
It leaves no flesh nor bones!
It is a thing that experts know,
that our furnaces are the best.

[*New melody*]
It is amazing what our people can do,
So obedient, diligently thrifty, and rational.
Yes say what you will about Gœthe's race,
but building crematorias, that they can do.

HERZ *exits*

■ SCENE 8

The Hotel Owner RAFAELE OMBRIOSO *enters, elegant and refined.*

RAFAELE: Good day.

FIDELE: Your highness deigns to descend to the gutter with us riff-raff. What has brought Your Grace to abandon the marbled halls of Hotel Dante.

PICCOLINO: Even a hotelier is made by God. Treat him as a human being.

All regard OMBRIOSO *hostilely.*

RAFAELE: The Bird Friends' delegation from Schweinsruhe will undertake an inspection tour through the town and will be moving towards the plaza.

All exit except FIDELE *and* RAFAELE *remaining.*

Marching music.

■ SCENE 9

RAFAELE: As chairman of the hunting club you are invited to a conference with the representatives of the Birds' Friends at seven o'clock this evening in the Hotel Dante. I, myself, will represent the Tourist Office. The Hunting Club really ought to send a representative. [FIDELE *nods*] Listen Fidele, we are both in the hotel industry; let's stand together. This can save us. [*They drink.*]

Scene shifts.

■ SCENE 10

At home with ROSA *and* CARUSO. *He lies on the sofa.* ROSA *sits on his lap. One sees both the interior of their home and the piazza.* MARCO *and* SANDRO *are idling out there. Bird posters are on the walls of the houses.*

ROSA: [*Laughing and singing*] A hunter is a beautiful thing! A hunter is a glorious thing. A hunter is a man. [*Pulls off his shoe.*] A hunter is a beautiful man. [*Pulls off his other shoe.*] A hunter is a glorious man. [*Takes off his jacket.*] The food is ready, with white beans. [*She rides up and down on his stomach*] You want to eat but I want something entirely different.

CARUSO: After dinner. [*She gets off. He sits at the table.*]

ROSA: I like hunters. [*She sits by the doorway to the street.*]

CARUSO: [*Drinking red wine from a beer glass and eating.*] The oil is good, sure, and the beans are good. [*Eats.*]

MARCO: I will never tolerate these hellish bird posters in our circolo. Never, never! Do you hear me!

SANDRO: You said something?

MARCO: These damned devilish shitty posters. And I will continue to hunt birds until I am so old that I can no longer see. You hear me!

CARUSO: Now I am coming to the birds, Rosa. Where's the pepper?

ROSA: In the cabinet.

CARUSO: [*Finding the pepper*] It smells excellent. I must not be interrupted now. [*Eats in silence.*]

ROSA: [*Sings*]

Jens Bjørneboe

"Oil Bread & Wine"

Say not who judges the case;
Who acts pure, who acts simple,
but rather when the rain comes

And tell me how is the wheat doing,
and tell how many bushels we will get,
and how the wine will be this year,
when the summer is over.

Olives grow on old trees.
They bear new fresh berries,
out of wheat comes bread and out of the grape
    the wine
and out of the berries the oil.

CARUSO: [*Gnawing on the bird*] The heads are the best. Crisp and fine.

■ SCENE 11

CAVALLI: [*Enters right*] Here they come.

SANDRO: [*Looks up*] Here?

CAVALLI: [*Pointing to the right*] Over there. [SANDRO *and* MARCO *get up.*]

MARCO: It is the whole delegation.

CAVALLI: [*Calling*] Fidele, they're coming!

■ SCENE 12

FIDELE: [*Enters left.*]. Are they here?

ROSA: [*Pointing*] There.

SANDRO, MARCO *and* CAVALLI *exit through the back.*

■ SCENE 13

RAFAELE'S VOICE: [*From off stage*] ...the Gozzi family's old tower was completed in 1292. The family began as wool merchants, accumulated an unparalleled fortune and built a bigger estate.

■ SCENE 14

RAFAELE, HULDREICH VON U. ZU GREIFENKLAU, MRS. STAHLMANN, MISS HERZ *and* JOHANNES *enter.*

RAFAELE: [*Pointing into the Salon.*] Ferro Castle was built after that, the family had gathered a fortune of 90 million gold florins, a lot of money at the time. [*All listen to him without a peep,* GREIFENKLAU *and* JOHANNES *smile piously.*] They had their own family chapel with a famous "Child Jesus" worth 150,000 marks and a worthy torture chamber with a "Jesus in the Temple" worth at least 200,000. Here in the tower we see before us a well from the middle of the 13th century where the rebel Antonio Pazzo was imprisoned for 13 years. When he was hauled up, he had raggedy hair and a beard down to his knees and moreover he had gone mad, supposedly because of his unhealthy brooding over social conditions. A miraculous well! [*Pointing to the Salon.*] In front of us lies the La Barcas family building with the Holy Family worth 300,000.

STAHLMANN: [*To* HERZ]They don't have a regular water closet. One must stand. Did you notice?

RAFAELE: The town hall has a pair of memorable beautifully crafted iron thumbscrews. [*Sees Fidele*] Do I have your permission? ....Restaurateur Fidele Pieno. Herr Greifenklau a member of the Justice Ministry in his homeland. Mrs. Director Stahlmann. Mr. Johannes Schulze treasurer of the Bird Lover's group. And Miss Herz who is...

CARUSO: [*In the door*] These are the goddam best larks I have ever eatten. Rosa you must...[*Stares at* GREIFENKLAU.]

HERZ: That is the horrible man I met in that dive. It's him.

CARUSO: [*Staring at* GREIFENKLAU] It's him.

RAFAELE: If the Ladies and Gentlemen will show the town and me the honor of following me. We will now inspect the first torture chamber in Palazzo Gozzi. [RAFAELE *and Bird Friends exit.*]

■ SCENE 15

CARUSO: Jesus Maria!

ROSA: What is it Caruso? You don't like the taste of the larks?

CARUSO *jumps past her, across the piazza and offstage in pursuit of the Bird Friends. He soon returns.*

CARUSO: [*Sings*]

Jens Bjørneboe

"Recognition Song"

Oh Great God in the heavens
Oh Jesus Maria and Marx and Lenin
I have seen him and knew him right away.
The Old Judge swine.
It is he.
  It is he.
    It is he.

It was the Judge and his lackey,
and neither of them recognized me.
When the Cat becomes the Mouse and the Mouse, the Cat,
that's when the night of the long knives comes.

Oh Great God in the heavens.
There they are, both the same men.
There was the Judge and his executing apprentice,
and I knew them both again.
It is they.
  It is they.
    It is they.

Oh Jesus Maria, Oh Holy Spirit,
You put them both in my hand.

When the Cat becomes the Mouse and the
Mouse, the Cat,
that's when the night of the long knives comes.

■ SCENE 16

ROSA: Caruso, what's with you?

CARUSO: [*Into the room*] Rosa!

ROSA: Are you sick?

CARUSO: Call the gang, Cavalli! Sandro! Marco! Piccolino! Quick! [ROSA *exits.*] Did you see them, Fidele?

FIDELE: Yes it was them.

CARUSO: So there really is a God!

■ SCENE 17

The others enter; SANDRO, MARCO, CAVALLI, PICCOLINO *and* ROSA.

CARUSO: Group "43" is activated. The alarm is ringing and we are in a state of emergency. You know what this means?

SANDRO: [*Standing at attention*] No, Captain.

CARUSO: The two men we talked about this morning, the Judge and his bailiff, have now come back here to...to receive justice.

MARCO: Is that true?

CARUSO: Fidele and I have seen them both.

Everyone in a vehement joyful outburst.

PICCOLINO: Well Caruso, Group '43' is once again called up. You have the command again. I bless you, my son.

EVERYONE: Hurrah! Hurrah! The day has come.

Vehement demonstration.

CARUSO: Fidele and Cavalli, go to the agreed upon meeting at the Hotel Dante at seven o'clock and discover exactly which room the Judge and his bailiff have. They should reside facing the terrace. Afterwards you both come here. Sandro, Marco, Father Piccolino and I will meet here at the same time as the conference in the hotel begins. Everyone should be armed and with weapons greased and overhauled. Is that clear?

MARCO: Check. [*Steps back.*]

SANDRO: Check. [*Steps back.*]

PICCOLINO: Check. [*Steps back.*]

FIDELE: Check. [*Steps back.*]

CAVALLI: Check. [*Steps back.*]

All in the Hunter's Club are singing and dancing with great abandon.

ALL: When the Cat becomes the Mouse and the Mouse, the Cat, that's when the night of the long knives comes.

Everyone exits. CARUSO *and* ROSA *alone. Lights Dim.*

SCENE 18

ROSA: What will you all do?

CARUSO: Justice. [*Takes rifle off of the wall.*]

ROSA: What is justice?

CARUSO: [*Kneels before the Virgin Mary Icon as he lifts the gun over his head.*] Holy Mother of God. Heavenly Queen. I swear that never more shall I hurt a feather of the song bird if You will shine Your grace over us today. Holy Virgin Mary, bless this gun.

Scene shifts

■ SCENE 19

Hotel Dante. The Salon. All the representatives of the Bird Lovers. Big intimidating bird posters on the walls. As we have already mentioned; a lot like the Occupying Powers' emblems.

GREIFENKLAU: These observations concerning fowl life go under the name of Pecker's law. When a single fowl becomes weak or sick the other fowl resolve to eliminate her and as though upon an agreed signal they gang up on her and peck her feathers off. Afterwards they peck out her eyes and when she starts bleeding they start pecking her where she bleeds. If the hen, for example, lays too big an egg such that she bleeds after the laying, they peck her from behind until they reach the guts and the intestines. They peck out all the intestines. The one hen jumps around blindly with all the others after her while the intestines are spilling out and trailing after her, often several meters. This speaks for itself that this answers to a deep and wise instinct that nature has implanted in all bird brains to preserve the health and normalcy of the race. [*The Bird Lovers set themselves up as a choir led by* JOHANNES *who nevertheless sings solo while he directs and brandishes a tuning fork or accompanies with a piano.*]

JOHANNES: We will do it again together with enthusiasm, then it will be really something.

"The Bird Lover's Song"

Nothing is so innocent as lovely birds.
You shall not hunt with powder and bullets.
The Birds whom we love
let them live free.

Listen to how they chirp and sing up in the trees.
They make our hearts so warm and sympathetic.
The Bird's heart is so gentle
let it beat secure and free!

The swallows in the heavens and the sparrows
on the field.

The magpies in the streets and the crows in the park,
Falcon and hawk and Mother Eagle,
Vultures, Ravens and Condors.

Mankind is evil but the birds are good.
Those who kill the birds, with them things will go bad.
Vultures, Ravens and Condors.
Falcon and hawk and Mother Eagle.

JOHANNES: Much better this time. But remember [*Sings*] Tia ta ti ta ta, isn't that so.

GREIFENKLAU: No. Ladies, the female never sings. The female only goes like this: grr, rr, grr, urrr, urrr, hurk, while the male however goes like this [*Whistles a few bars of bird song*]. That is something else again. When the female does "grr, rrr, urrk, hurrk!" one can't really call that singing. Right, Johan?

JOHANNES: Of course not, Herr Doctor.

HERZ: Can you encore your charming song, Herr Doctor?

GREIFENKLAU: And this, my friends, is a typical nightingale motif; a strophe and an anti-strophe

[*Whistles*] "Kuirri—vitt-kuirri-uitt-pyi-pyi-pyi-pu."

STAHLMANN: You really capture it, Herr Doctor.

GREIFENKLAU: Several typical black bird tones; "Pui-pui-pui-uhui-uhu-uhu-uhu" and so on. The female has only "purr prr prr rrkrrk krr rrk." You hear it Madame?

STAHLMANN: If only I could do it! It is good enough that we women do what we can. The cakes, Herz! We have a vertible surprise for you today, Herr Doctor. Also for you, Johannes. Herr Doctor *loves* apple pie, rich apple pie. Home baked from Schweinsruhe.

GREIFENKLAU: Apple pie!

STAHLMANN: Apple pie.

GREIFENKLAU: Home baked?

STAHLMANN: Home baked.

GREIFENKLAU: From Schweinsruhe?

STAHLMANN: We had it with us the whole way, Herr Doctor. For your sake. Ring for the apple pie,

Herz. Rafaele will bring it in.

HERZ: [*Ringing.*] I believe Rafaele is Jewish.

STAHLMANN: Yet he is so sweet and lovely.

Herz rings again.

Long pause.

JOHANNES: Yes, there are still some of them down here.

STAHLMANN: Yes to be sure but first and foremost there is the need for new sewage and water pipes and naturally the whole system of hygiene. Ban the handling of fruit and vegetables without rubber gloves and be sure to boil the water.

JOHANNES: In the old days there were certainly masses of them here.

SCENE 20

RAFAELE *enters with tea and apple pie.*

GREIFENKLAU: Oh no, real apple pie.

RAFAELE: [*Bowing deeply*] My ladies and gentlemen.

STAHLMANN: I just told the friends here what a shame it is that you have not seen Herr Doctor's magnificent villa in Schweinsruhe with the flower gardens and the charming birds! There is a layout that must have cost almost a half a million.

GREIFENKLAU: More, more. [*Eats the pie*] A lot more.

STAHLMANN: Herr Doctor now and then whistles all kinds of bird melodies. Only ask him for which one.

RAFAELE: Canary.

GREIFENKLAU: [*Chews and swallows*] Only the hen sings! First a sick hen: "ihi…ihi…ihi." That's nothing. They squeak with a high thin voice. Now comes a healthy hen with a beautiful deep voice: "Orr, orr,orr" and so on. The canary population has suffered awful reversals here in this area. The stock is good but imports are banned. New blood does not get in. *We* could get new blood out of our own breeders back home in Schweinsruhe, the purest and finest blood. The best race in the world for voice and color! Color! Race! We could deliver 15,000 immediately. Would you cooperate? As the inspector you would receive over 20%.

RAFAELE: It would be a very great pleasure. I shall now

bring good news.

GREIFENKLAU: Listen everyone! The Hotel director brings good news.

RAFAELE: The local hunting club has been practical enough to recognize the hunting ban. Coming face to face with the ironclad realities they have to all intents and purposes given in.

Silence.

HERZ: No more song birds will be shot!

STAHLMANN: Never again will little birds be hurt.

JOHANNES: Never again will they be eaten.

■ SCENE 21

SERVANT: [*Opens door.*] The delegates from the hunting club.

STAHLMANN: A hearty welcome. [CAVALLI *and* FIDELE *enter*] Here is an apple pie with poppy seed.

CAVALLI: We're here to be as tough as you.

FIDELE: Hunting is an old tradition in this district.

STAHLMANN: Was.

CAVALLI: We won't yield an inch.

STAHLMANN: We're not giving up a millimeter.

FIDELE: Hunting is our ancient right.

STAHLMANN: Now we are here!

JOHANNES: We assert our rights.

HERZ: Have you no empathy with creation, with small helpless birds, our singing brothers?

GREIFENKLAU: The nightingale, the thrush, the lark?

JOHANNES: We represent thousands and ten thousands of bird lovers, and not only that, but animal lovers and animal protectors throughout all of our great fatherland—millions.

FIDELE: We'll continue to hunt.

JOHANNES: [*Bellowing*] We are 60 million bird lovers.

HERZ: [*Very mild*] The small defenseless winged beings.

You have a heart to do *that*?

RAFAELE: Hunting has hardly any value compared to the tourist traffic; and...

STAHLMANN: ...they will stay away from now on.

RAFAELE: Without the hunting ban, no resort town.

JOHANNES: [*Loudly*] We are a humane people. We have always been humane towards the animals.

HERZ: Can we not speak to your hearts? 100,000 marks.

STAHLMANN: They have no hearts. Only we have feelings.

CAVALLI: It is true that the tourist traffic is an undeniably big deal.

FIDELE: Don't even listen to them.

GREIFENKLAU: Don't bother them with arguments. You force us to use power. I detest violence. But we are millions of bird lovers.

JOHANNES: Each year 4 million of our countrymen come here as tourists. Each bird friend leaves hundreds, thousands of marks. We demand that hunting be stopped. We find it intolerable. Unbearable.

FIDELE: [*Hesitantly*] Hunting is our only pleasure.

GREIFENKLAU: You have our offer. We will create a resort town here at Torre Rosse with the collective capacity of around 2000 guests at a time, up to about 20,000 visitors a year. Each of them will spend at the very least 1,000 marks in a year. That adds up to 20 million. If hunting is not forbidden not only will you get not even a glimpse of that but also you will lose all other tourist traffic from us. It is a huge loss.

FIDELE: We can find a compromise. We hunt 6 months of the year.

STAHLMANN: Not allowed.

HERZ: Denied.

JOHANNES: Unthinkable.

CAVALLI: Three months.

GREIFENKLAU: No conditions.

FIDELE: It is our country.

STAHLMANN: It is our money.

FIDELE: Restricted hunting for three months of the year and only in certain areas.

JOHANNES: Unthinkable. It will only terrify the birds.

GREIFENKLAU: It will destroy them.

CAVALLI: We are determined.

FIDELE: I stand firm. Restricted hunting.

STAHLMANN: All or nothing.

FIDELE: This is our hunt. Our town!

JOHANNES: Morality is on our side.

GREIFENKLAU: The loss will be unimaginable.

RAFAELE: We have no remedy for that, Fidele.

CAVALLI: The cost is too high.

FIDELE: Then I can only wish the Schweinsruhe chapter of the Bird Lover's Group division of the Land's Office of Animal Protection welcome to Torre Rosse. A hearty welcome here from us.

STAHLMANN: You have the mandate to choose the hunting club's path?

FIDELE: Yes.

GREIFENKLAU: The case is closed.

HERZ: Have a piece of apple pie. I learned to bake this pie for the soldiers during the war. We collected day old pies and cakes and used books and wool blankets and shoes and clothing for our poor wounded in the field hospitals.

CAVALLI: That's something I can sing about;

"The Lazarette Song"

Christmas nineteen and forty one
was celebrated with courage.
All the men in our ward
got brand new bandages.

The packages came from near and far
from housewife and girl,
with books, stockings, shoes and clothes
and things that should please everyone.

Benno got a book or two.
Giovanni cake and candy.

Carlo got a pair of new shoes.
Michele got some mittens.

Benno was as blind as a stone,
Giovanni was missing his guts.
Carlo had no legs,
and Michele no arms.

FIDELE: You certainly must have heard the nightingales here, already.

JOHANNES: We will leave tomorrow morning.

GREIFENKLAU: Tonight we must hear them. Aj aj aj. Oh for the pleasure of hearing the pure angel tones again.

CAVALLI: It depends somewhat on which room you gentlemen will get in the hotel.

FIDELE: It depends entirely on where one is.

GREIFENKLAU: You can't hear it the same everywhere?

CAVALLI: There are big differences.

JOHANNES: This is very good to find out.

GREIFENKLAU: Oh Herr Director! Ombrioso! How

is it with our rooms. Will we hear the nightingale well?

JOHANNES: The two gentlemen from the hunting club mentioned that there was a great difference.

FIDELE: As old hunters we know where the birds are.

GREIFENKLAU: Of course. Herr Ombrioso I will certainly want to record the singing tonight.

RAFAELE: I have not thought about this consideration. The gentlemen are booked on the 2nd floor.

CAVALLI: Damn! That's awkward.

FIDELE: You're right. No balcony entrance.

RAFAELE: I hadn't really thought about that.

GREIFENKLAU: [*To* CAVALLI] Where do you think one will hear the nightingales best?

CAVALLI: Yep, what do you say, Fidele? Facing the ocean and the stand of pine trees?

FIDELE: The terrace.

CAVALLI: The terrace. Absolutely!

RAFAELE: On the first floor?

CAVALLI: The first floor with the big French windows.

FIDELE: Opposite the ocean and the pine trees. Absolutely.

GREIFENKLAU: Do you believe, Mr. Ombrioso, that you could be so kind.

RAFAELE: Of course. It is done in a moment. I will give the order at once. Both gentlemen?

JOHANNES: Yes, yes, me too. [RAFAELE *exits.*]

CAVALLI: The windows should, of course, be opened.

GREIFENKLAU: Naturally.

CAVALLI: [*To* JOHANNES] The windows...the big French windows must be opened. Otherwise one doesn't hear a thing.

FIDELE: Not a thing.

GREIFENKLAU: Do you think it will go well tonight?

FIDELE: By the moonlight you can judge that it will be a fine dark night. Ideal.

CAVALLI: Very dark. As though we had ordered it.

RAFAELE: [*Returns*] It is done. The gentlemen's bags are being sent down.

CAVALLI: It is not too near the street? That would be disturbing.

RAFAELE: No, no it is 3 and 5. The closest to the trees.

CAVALLI: That's good.

■ SCENE 22

Dim light at CARUSO AND ROSA'S. SANDRO, MARCO, PATER PICCOLINO, CARUSO *and* ROSA. *The street outside is obscured in darkness. The men are armed.*

MARCO: Finally something is being done, all right.

PICCOLINO: Nothing can be done. We haven't done anything yet. Fools.

ROSA: You will be arrested and exposed. You will be caught all of you. Jesus Maria what a collection of idiots. Lord God protect them. What an idiot I have married. You frog, you fools. Oh God in heaven if they take you now. Are you listening?! You feeble minded old tom cat. Lord Jesus take care of him! Idiots! You are risking your lives. [*Shakes him violently.*] Cretins.

CARUSO: [*Wakes up and reaches for the rifle.*] Did they come?

ROSA: You were sleeping while I was talking to you?! You beast!

CARUSO: If I should stay awake as long as you are able to talk, then I will never grow old.

ROSA: You rat, you dumb rabbit. Lord God you must be careful, my love.

CARUSO: [*Looks at the clock.*] Have you been talking the whole time?

ROSA: You think nothing of your wives and children. Only of yourselves. Let go of your idiotic firearms. Drop them to the floor!

PICCOLINO: Sssh. I hear something.

ROSA: You should all be in bed sleeping now, imbeciles. Tomorrow you won't be able to work. Idiots.

CARUSO: You have inspired us enough, Rosa.

ROSA: Let go of your rifles. At once, cretins!

In the outside darkness, there is a glimpse of two shapes. There are knocks at the door.

CARUSO: Who is it?

VOICE: "43"

CARUSO: All clear. [CAVALLI *and* FIDELE *enter.*] What's the situation?

SCENE 23

FIDELE: Number 3 and 5. First floor opposite the terrace.

CARUSO: Good. [*Everybody gets up.*] Then Piccolino and Fidele together. Marco and I together. Sandro and Cavalli give the all clear in the Circolo. The ropes and everything. You wait there. Is that clear?

SANDRO: [*Slings the rifle and bandolier over his shoulder.*] Check. [*Exits.*]

ROSA: You stay here! Stop!

CAVALLI: [*Takes the rifle and bandolier.*] Check. [*Exits.*]

ROSA: You dare not! Oh God protect you. Maria help them. [PICCOLINO *and* FIDELE *take their things, nod and go.*] You stay here. Jesus where will this end. Riff raff, bandits, idiots, Jesus and Maria! Cretins, won't you stay here? [CARUSO *and* MARCO *grab their things. She flings herself around his neck and holds him.*] Stay here! My Darling! Don't go. Idiot! It is a sin to kill people. Stay here.

CARUSO: People! Away from me, woman. [*Pulls her off.*]

ROSA: It is so stupid that it is laughable.

CARUSO: "Laughable!" The men who killed my brother and your husband! After today the hunting ban goes into effect.

ROSA: Maria save them. Help them. Cursed idiots! [*The men exit.*] Don't be late! Come right home after the murders, Caruso! You have to get up early tomorrow. Holy Mother of God, save them. [*To the audience.*] So that's the way it is. We can be used to wash the dishes, to scrub the floor, to wash the clothes. We can be used when there is a war to smuggle food and weapons and to dress the wounds. We can be used to sit in jail. But when you are about to kill who asks us then? Who asks what we want? [*In front of Maria's Icon.*]

"The Rosa Song"

Of all the Lord's blessings,
Peace is our greatest gift.
Oh forgive us Mother of God
for what is going to happen tonight.

Oh listen to our prayers.
Bless and redeem every soul.
Now our men and sons
are going out to kill.

And there are those who strike down their brothers.
And there are those who have no bread.
Oh holy Mother of God,
tonight there are those who shall die.

PART II

■ SCENE 24

GREIFENKLAU *in his hotel room. The Bird Poster with the eagles depicted just like the old occupation emblem. Door windows stand half open. He sets up a tape recorder, goes to the door and opens it.*

JOHANNES: [*Enters*] Herr Doctor?

GREIFENKLAU: [*Takes off his jacket.*] The collar. [JOHANNES *loosens and removes his collar and tie.* GREIFENKLAU *sits down and holds his foot out.* JOHANNES *kneels before him and pulls off his boots.*] Just think, we're in this corner of the world again. Johannes....

JOHANNES: Oh yes Herr Doctor.

GREIFENKLAU: Isn't it remarkable to be back here? It is like a kind of rapture. The place has an attraction...like goosebumps, a kind of trembling.

JOHANNES: Yes I am quivering, Herr Doctor. Quivering.

GREIFENKLAU: You who are a singing teacher and musician, as a spiritual cultured person....

JOHANNES: And you, a member of the Justice ministry. Yes, yes. [*Gives him an imploring look.*]

GREIFENKLAU: Times have changed...yet all remains the same. What is it?

JOHANNES: Do I have permission, sir. The shirt? [GREIFENKLAU *lifts his arms.*]

JOHANNES: [*Takes his shirt off.*] So, Herr Doctor, so.

GREIFENKLAU: Thank you, my boy. Yes, yes. It was the time of the court martials. We did a tough job, you and I.

JOHANNES: Thank you Herr Doctor. Do I have permission. The undershirt? Thank you. It was you Herr Doctor who deserves the credit.

GREIFENKLAU: Ah oh. [*Undershirt pulled over his head.*] Ah oh [*Stretches his foot forward.*] The stockings, Johannes. Thanks my boy. Yes it was in the old days. [JOHANNES *pulls his stockings off. It is a long lady's silk stocking.*] We did our duty. That was all. As our fathers before us. Our duty as soldiers.

JOHANNES: [*Hanging the stockings carefully over the chair's back.*] It was a time of great Destiny, with demanding and important work. The arrests. The deportations. The interrogations. The sweat poured off of me all the time. And the pogroms. The awesome pogroms. It was great to know that I worked for the Fatherland.

GREIFENKLAU: For the Fatherland.

BOTH: *The Fatherland!*

JOHANNES: [*Sings*]

"SS Camp Song"

Moses was a Jewish scamp,
with a nose almost a foot long.
You meet a Jewish rascal,
spit on him in the puss.

BOTH:

Heil Hitler in our fatherland!
From all the land and coast.
The women in the ghetto
have yard long breasts.

JOHANNES:

You meet a Jewish scum,

knock him down like lightning.
You see some Jewish shit,
kick him in the teeth.

BOTH:

Heil Hitler in our fatherland!
From all the land and coast.
The women in the ghetto
have yard long breasts.

JOHANNES:

And when you meet a Jewish pack,
then kick them in the crotch.
Jewish swine and polack shits
we don't permit to live.

GREIFENKLAU:

SS is well known everywhere
as saints with glory.
Belsen, Auschwitz, Buchenwald
have superb crematories.

BOTH:

Heil Hitler in our fatherland!
From all the land and coast.
The women in the ghetto
have yard long breasts.

JOHANNES:

And we who have something just right
for such shit scum.
We turn on a dose of gas
and listen to them scream.

BOTH:

Jews and gypsy shits
with their young and their wives.
The Ovens have the appetite
for many millions.

GREIFENKLAU: Yes. Yes. They claim 6 million. It's the mustache clipper.

JOHANNES: [*Helps with the mustache clipper.*] I believe it is propaganda, Herr Justice Councillor. It was hardly more than five.

GREIFENKLAU: At the very most five. [*Holds his arms out.*] It's my corset. [JOHANNES *unfastens it.*] You still work for the fatherland, my boy. [*Slaps him.*] In your capacity as a teacher. When you teach your students to do their duty, that's when you are still a fighter for the fatherland, for the fatherland's *economy*. Work and duty, Johannes.

JOHANNES: Thank you Herr Doctor. [*Struggles with the corset.*]

GREIFENKLAU: You can call me General, Johannes. I still have a General's rank. As in the old days. From the last year of the War.

JOHANNES: [*Removes corset.*] Thank you very much, Herr General. I think often about the travels through the countries, all the legal actions and judgments. We condemned many.

GREIFENKLAU: The mustache clipper isn't working right. [*Goes to wash up.*] The executions were justified, Johannes. Help me with the clipper. It is too bushy.

SANDRO: No it's that one is higher than the other. Must adjust it.

JOHANNES: [*Helps.*] Now it is just like the old days. The last executions were, of course, dangerous. Right! So now it fits, Herr General. Can we soon say Herr Justice Minister?

GREIFENKLAU: Presumably. The cabinet post seems to be more than just a rumor.

JOHANNES: Is it that close? Many had to undergo a lengthy examination before they confessed.

GREIFENKLAU: I have never underestimated your work

as Examining Officer. There is just something on the neck. There's the razor. You were superb.

JOHANNES: [*Shaving his neck.*] It is incredible what people can withstand in an examination before they confess. Hold still, Herr General.

GREIFENKLAU: Yes I know many held out for a long time. But with you they found their match. I have not forgotten that. Soon I will acknowledge that.

JOHANNES: Thank you, Herr General. [CARUSO'S *face pops up in the window.*]

GREIFENKLAU: Today I have my General's rank in an even greater military alliance. Our former enemies have had to acknowledge our position as a great power. Economically we are today three times as strong as the last time. And there are many behind us. Our military alliance regards us as Europe's defender. Thank you, my friend. It is excellent. There, you see the tape recorder. I'll tape the nightingale tonight.

JOHANNES: I just heard something outside, on the terrace. [*Puts away the barbering tools and wipes his neck.*] If you will, Herr General.

GREIFENKLAU: Probably a cat. [*The nightingale is heard outside.*] Thank you my friend.

JOHANNES: I hope it is not on the prowl. On a night like this all of nature should be at peace. [*Nightingale.*]

GREIFENKLAU: That's right. Now, I must be alone, my boy. Good night.

JOHANNES: Sleep well, Herr General. [*Exits.*]

■ SCENE 25

The Nightingale sings again. GREIFENKLAU *locks the door and starts the tape recorder. He opens the suitcase and pulls out a case from which he takes a heavy whip. He sits down and listens more and more entranced with the bird's song. Finally he is ecstatic. He turns off the tape recorder and whips himself on the back while he groans deeply. Afterwards he relaxes.*

■ SCENE 26

CARUSO *and* FIDELE *quietly come in through the balcony window, both masked and armed.*

GREIFENKLAU: Good evening, gentlemen. Two armed young men against an old unarmed man. Sure, sure. Help yourself.

CARUSO: If you shout we will shoot at once.

GREIFENKLAU: I don't doubt it. There's my suitcase and there in my jacket is my wallet. Help yourself. There hangs the camera. On the table is my herbarium which hardly has any value for you. And the traveller's checks you cannot countersign. Voila, gentlemen.

CARUSO: Get dressed.

GREIFENKLAU: You don't understand? There is what I have with me. Damn you and get out. I'll summon the police as soon as you are gone. But you'll have a few minutes head start and a sporting chance to escape your fate. But spare me from seeing you for much longer in here.

CARUSO: You will get dressed or I will shoot you here.

GREIFENKLAU: Do you think that you can scare me? You! A thief! A man of my age! An Officer! [*They aim their rifles at him.*] Go ahead, shoot. You think this is the first time I've stood in front of a rifle's muzzle? The gentlemen are exceptionally bold.

Remarkably courageous—What is it you want with me?

CARUSO: You will be with us tonight. Shoes, jacket, hat, quickly!

GREIFENKLAU: Dare I ask what the gentlemen want with me?

CARUSO: To take you or shoot you here.

GREIFENKLAU: A ha! I believe you. It is a laughable idea, to give me orders.

FIDELE: If you come with us you have a chance to survive.

GREIFENKLAU: What do you mean "to survive." Ha, ha, ha.

FIDELE: If you come along perhaps you will live tomorrow.

GREIFENKLAU: Then I must really request my two courteous young guests to shoot an unarmed man at once. Be so good! The gentlemen shall not be hindered. Be right at home. You don't dare to shoot at once! [CARUSO *lifts his shotgun and sticks it in* GREIFENKLAU'S *face.*] Let me permit myself to explain that the gentlemen are mongrels. The gentlemen are what I as an officer must describe as bastards. They believe that they can give orders to an *officer*. An officer, my friends, who has fought in two world wars. A man who in his time spent four years in the trenches of the Western Front. I have survived Verdun. I have fought on the Sommes. I have eaten the mud of Chemin des Dames. *Do you understand what it is to say one has survived Verdun*!

[*To the audience.*] Hartmannswyler Kopp! Do you know that just 25 years later in the Battle of Hartmannswyler Kopp in WW II the dead of WW I came up again from the graves under fire. To be sure only the skeletons but this shows in all events how many were buried close together there.

[*Sings as a French Chanson.*]

"Chanson about Verdun"

Oh Sommes and Verdun and Chemin des Dames
Oh Filth and Mud and Blood and Dirt.
Oh Chemin des Dames! Oh Chemin des Dames!
Oh names from my forgotten youth.

In Marne and Verdun and in No Man's Land.
In Clay and Mud and Slime and Water.
There lies the three million men

and all lie there still.

In Chemin des Dames and Verdun and Marne
It has rained for a hundred years
and Summer turns into Fall and Winter into
Spring.
There it rained in my youth.

In No Man's Land of Verdun and Sommes
There drowned in Mud everyone who comes
In Chemin des Dames and Verdun and Sommes,
there we drowned in sludge.

On the Marne and in Hartmannswyler Kopp
there the Dead constantly came up,
for in Hartmannswyler Kopp
it was very full of the Dead.

And all the young boys from all the countries,
they met in Flanders and in Alsace.
We had unfortunately too little room
for five million small boys.

We buried them for three years
by Chemin des Dames and in No Man's Land.
In the 4th year there was peace.
And there were still some living.

I went to Death's kingdom and was resurrected in the 4th year from the Dead. [*To* CARUSO.] What do you know about resurrection? I have undoubtedly lived long enough. Please shoot!

FIDELE: Do you have a wife and children, my Herr?

GREIFENKLAU: Yes, yes, a wife. And children. They are grown now.

FIDELE: You have small grandchildren back home?

GREIFENKLAU: Yes, fairly small.... Very little, very sweet children [*Thinks.*] They will do well enough without some twitching old timer around.

CARUSO: I remind you that you have duties towards them.

GREIFENKLAU: I have no duties any longer. [*Roaring.*] I have my honor as an Officer. How does that concern you?

FIDELE: You have your roses and your birds? You have animals and flowers at home. I permit myself to mention that, Signore.

GREIFENKLAU: [*Softly.*] Yes, yes. [*His head sinks.*] Animals and flowers.

FIDELE: You have your chores and your occupations, your work in the regiment's archives and in the Justice Ministry. Do you understand? I'll remind you of the life insurance, the pension, policies for your grandchildren? And I assume that you are clear as to what this [*Points to* CARUSO *and himself.*] is about?

GREIFENKLAU: Yes. [*Nods.*]

FIDELE: I permit myself, Signore, to mention a bank account for the grandchildren.

GREIFENKLAU [*Thinks very slowly.*] I'll go along.

CARUSO: Thank you, Signore. [*While they lower their guns, he puts on the necessities.*]

GREIFENKLAU: This is ridiculous and I'll mention that I despise you. [*Continues dressing.*] I'm ready. Where are we going?

CARUSO: [*Nods to the terrace window.*] After you, Signore.

GREIFENKLAU: Thank you [*Looks about stiff and disdainfully.*] The gentlemen misunderstand me if you believe I wish to live forever. I assure you, you have my most open contempt. [*All exit.*]

■ SCENE 27

"Circolo" set up as a courtroom. From the roof beams hang two ropes tied into hangman's nooses. Underneath a plank rests between two boxes. The windows and doors are barricaded. Bird Posters. Rifles. SANDRO *and* CAVALLI.

SANDRO: You remember Corona? The little bordello by the cinema?

CAVALLI: The bordello was good. Not the wine.

SANDRO: The cheese was good.

CAVALLI: Alborno! That was a wine...ah!

SANDRO: [*Nods.*] The bad bordellos.

CAVALLI: La Spezia.

SANDRO: The bordellos...good.

CAVALLI: The wine good.

SANDRO: The cheese fair.

CAVALLI: The fish good.

SANDRO: In Marseilles the fish was good.

CAVALLI: The wine remarkable.

SANDRO: The bordellos miserable.

CAVALLI: In Cremona they had comfortable brothels.

SANDRO: Yes that little one behind the church of the Virgin Mary. It was like being home. The food was good.

CAVALLI: The wine was fine.

SANDRO: The white.

CAVALLI: Leone?

SANDRO: The food good.

CAVALLI: The wine good.

SANDRO: The bordellos terrible.

CAVALLI: Naples.

SANDRO: A lot of garlic.

CAVALLI: The wine?

SANDRO: Good.

CAVALLI: The bordellos?

SANDRO: Good.

CAVALLI: Naples is a fine city.

SANDRO: [*Pointing at a rope.*] I can't stand seeing that it hangs wrong.

CAVALLI: What's that?

SANDRO: The one on the right.

CAVALLI: [*Points*] That one there?

SANDRO: No to the right.

CAVALLI: That one is *on* the right!

SANDRO: As I see it that one is on the right. I can't bear to see it so. If one is longer than the other it gets on my nerves.

CAVALLI: It is not that one is shorter than the other.

SANDRO: No it's that one is higher than the other. Must adjust it. Come here and look. [CAVALLI *joins him. They pull on the ropes together.*]

CAVALLI: They must be even.

SANDRO: Stay here, I'll fix it. [*Brings a stepladder and climbs up to the roof beam.*] Is it better?

CAVALLI: A little more.

SANDRO: Like this.

CAVALLI: Little more. No. Stop.

SANDRO: Is it right now?

CAVALLI: No lower. That's too much. Let it down.

SANDRO: So.

CAVALLI: A little bit more ....

SANDRO: Is it there?

CAVALLI: A little up again.

SANDRO: There.

CAVALLI: Just a little. So!

SANDRO: [*Down to* CAVALLI.] Now that's neat.

CAVALLI: Must you always have it down to the millimeter?

SANDRO: Always. Have you lathered it well?

CAVALLI: Black head shampoo.

SANDRO: It makes me jumpy just to see it hanging like that. [*He takes away the ladder.*] A drink.

CAVALLI: Red wine. [*They go to the bar together.*] It is going well, this. [*They drink. A knock at the door.*]

CAVALLI: It's them.

SANDRO: [*Drinks up.*] Hrrm. Who is it?

A VOICE: "43"

They go to the door and lift the bar.

CAVALLI: Here.

He opens the door halfway. Johannes is pushed in and falls on the floor. He remains on his knees. MARCO *and* PICCOLINO *enter after him, keeping their guns on him.*

SCENE 28

MARCO: Here we have the swine. He who led the execution squad. [*Playacts.*] Ready, aim, fire.

JOHANNES: You have the wrong man. I have never in my life ever done anyone harm.

MARCO: Shut up.

JOHANNES: [*Still on his knees.*] Don't aim at me. Take them away.

MARCO: Stop your yapping. [*Points at the ropes.*] Look at that.

JOHANNES: [*Crawling on the floor.*] Help. Help. What are you going to do with them? God! Lord God!

MARCO: Exactly, *that* is what we're going to do with them. But first we'll put you through a regular trial. Here it is going to be perfectly correct for you. No one shall be punished without a judgment. No one shall...what is the rest of it, Piccolino?

PICCOLINO: We have taken justice into our own hands without formalities but after the spirit of justice.

JOHANNES: Holy Father. God in heaven is my witness that I have never been here before. You have the wrong man. I cry to God that I never....

CAVALLI: If you don't shut up now you'll get the same treatment before we hang you as you gave Benjamino and Caruso and his Pole before they were shot.

JOHANNES: I swear that it was not me. Give me a Bible to swear on. It must be someone who looked like me.

CAVALLI: He gave Caruso a disciplinary punishment before he would shoot him. You pig, you were always beating.

PICCOLINO: He is not judged yet. He should be treated as if he was innocent.

MARCO: Is that how he treated us?

JOHANNES: I am a singing teacher.

PICCOLINO: Set him down in the corner and guard him. Sandro, take care of it.

SANDRO: [*Pulls* JOHANNES *to set him down under one of the Bird posters.*] There, don't move. [*Sits down and keeps his gun on him.*]

JOHANNES: Lord Jesus in heaven. [*Weeps loudly.*]

CAVALLI: [*To* MARCO *and* PICCOLINO.] The ropes hang well, what?

MARCO: They should be a little higher. What do you say, Holy Father?

PICCOLINO: Yeah. It is as we use to have them. The boxes. Are you sure that you can stand on them?

CAVALLI: [*Demonstrating*] They're solid. You only have to kick them away and presto; there.

JOHANNES: [*Sobbing*] Release me. Let me go home....

SANDRO: One more word, so!....

JOHANNES: Singing teacher.

MARCO: It is taking a long time with Caruso and Fidele. They're late. [*Looks at* JOHANNES.] If you are a singing teacher so you can sing for us by gosh. Sing!

SANDRO: [*Threatening*] Sing something. [*They surround him.*] Sing a song.

CAVALLI: Sing something cheerful!

SANDRO: [*Lifting his rifle stock over him.*] Sing!

EVERYONE: Sing. [*They force him to sing.*]

JOHANNES: [*Singing.*]

"The Soldier Song"

The melody is a catchy march with each strophe opening with a drumroll. The last two lines in each verse is sung to the tune of "Lily Marlene."

We march. We destroy.
We march the soldier's way
from Moscow to Paris,
from Karasjouk to Arles and Nice,
Dunkirk and Tripoli.
Before Stalingrad there stands a battalion,
the remnants of our best division.

We march and we master,
we conquer and march,
From Cairo up to Hammarfest.
From Brussels up to Budapest
From Copenhagen to Bucharest.
Before Leningrad there stands a cannon
the remnants of our last battalion.

We march. We destroy.
We master Czechslovakia,
Vichy and Algeria,
Hungary, Luxemborg and the Hague.
In Denmark and in Prague.
Up in the Karels lies a pair of skies
the remnants of our last company.

We march. We destroy.
We devastate and we conquer.
We march through the storm and snow.
From Smolensk to Calais
From Omsk to Zuder Zee.
Back home in Dresden there stands a doorway,
the remnant of our last cathedral.

Knocking on the door. JOHANNES *almost falls off the chair. Everyone else stands up.*

CAVALLI: Who is it?

A VOICE: "43"

CAVALLI: Here.

They open up. FIDELE, CARUSO *and* GREIFENKLAU *enter.* FIDELE *has his gun barrel on the Doctor's back.*

■ SCENE 29

GREIFENKLAU: Don't rush me. [*Looks about.*] Six men, what? Ha, ha, ha!

JOHANNES: Herr Doctor, these men are anarchists.

GREIFENKLAU: So, so my boy. Calm yourself. Even though we are few.

PICCOLINO: When we last met, Herr Doctor, you were in control.

GREIFENKLAU: In the name of Law and Justice. There really is a difference .

FIDELE: You are standing in a courtroom now also, Herr District Attorney, but this time as the accused. There's the difference.

GREIFENKLAU: Ha. [*Looks about.*] Ha, ha, ha. A courtroom. With a mandate from whom? From. . . .

JOHANNES: God, Herr Doctor. God!

GREIFENKLAU: Ssssh.

FIDELE: A tribunal of the Partisans from these mountains. A military tribunal.

GREIFENKLAU: Military, ha, ha.

PICCOLINO: I was a guerrilla priest for three years. For your sake, Herr Doctor, I must draw your attention to the fact that this proceeding is not a joke. You are under indictment for murder.

JOHANNES: Oh Lord Jesus!

FIDELE: Furthermore for gross assault and abuse.

JOHANNES: [*Sobbing loudly*] Mur… mur… murder.

GREIFENKLAU: I will allow myself to smile. I smile. [*Silence.*]

CARUSO: As Captain I have summoned group "43" to active service. The accused will take their places. [GREIFENKLAU *takes his place above* JOHANNES.] Are the following in their places; Marco, Chauffeur?

MARCO: Here.

CARUSO: Sandro Vitale, farm worker?

SANDRO: Here.

CARUSO: Fidele Pieno, restaurateur?

FIDELE: Here.

CARUSO: Cavallo Cavalli, men and women hair dresser.

CAVALLI: Here.

CARUSO: Piccolino Michelangelo, ordained priest of the Holy Roman Catholic church, priest for all eternity?

PICCOLINO: Here.

CARUSO: Marco Pazzi are you willing for this court session to act as bailiff and guard?

MARCO: Yes sir!

CARUSO: As the Court's foreman I ask if the following are ready to assume the task of jurors: Sandro Vitale.

SANDRO: Yes sir. [*Takes his place behind the bench.*]

CARUSO: Fidele Pieno.

FIDELE: Yes sir. [*Takes his place.*]

CARUSO: Cavallo Cavalli.

CAVALLI: Yes. [*Takes his place.*]

CARUSO: Father Michelangelo.

PICCOLINO: Yes sir. [*Takes his place.*]

The Trial

CARUSO: The court is in session.

GREIFENKLAU: Ha.

CARUSO: Respect for the court. [*Gavels.*]

GREIFENKLAU: I demand to abandon this venue. I am an officer and a member of the Justice Ministry in my....

CARUSO: You can just try to abandon the venue. Officer of the Day, Marco Pazzi, through his operations in the mountains, has shot 143 soldiers and 38 officers from which 9 with major's rank or higher. Has the accused more to say?

GREIFENKLAU: Pah! [*Remains standing.*]

CARUSO: Court's charge to the jury: Because this court of law can not return a sentence of imprisonment therefore it will only return a verdict of guilty or not guilty punishable by death that cannot be overruled by another court of law. The members of the court will also execute the sentence. The judge is the executioner and the executioner is the judge. [*Rises.*] Defendant Number 1 doctor juris Huldreich von und zu Greifenklau is accused of the murder of Janusz Swiderski and Benjamino Verde, done in the town of Bonzo, March 11th 1943. Also for the attempted murder of Caruso Gentile same time and place. Also for contributing to the grave abuse of Rosa Verde, Benjamino Verde, Janusz Swiderski and Caruso Gentile same time and place, also for the illegal deprivation of the freedom of these people same time and place. Defendant Number 2 music and gymnastic teacher Johannes Schulze is accused of the murder of Janusz Swiderski and Benjamino Verde, done in the town of Bonzo, March 11th 1943. Also for the attempted murder of Caruso Gentile same time and place. Further for the grave abuse of Rosa Verde, Benjamino Verde, Janusz Swiderski and Caruso Gentile same time and place.

Defendant Number 1 are you guilty or not guilty of the accusation?

GREIFENKLAU: Not guilty.

CARUSO: Defendant Number 2 are you guilty or not guilty of the accusation? [JOHANNES *will not answer.*]

GREIFENKLAU: Lift your head, man!

JOHANNES: Not guilty.

CARUSO: Defendant Number 1 were you in the town of Bonzo at the mentioned time; March 11th, 1943?

GREIFENKLAU: Yes.

CARUSO: In what capacity were you there?

GREIFENKLAU: Judge and State Advocate in the military court.

CARUSO: Thank you. Defendant Number 2 were you in the town of Bonzo at the same time; March 11th, 1943?

JOHANNES: No, absolutely not.

GREIFENKLAU: The truth!

JOHANNES: I was there.

CARUSO: In what capacity?

JOHANNES: As Herr Doctor's personal orderly and assistant.

CARUSO: Nothing more?

GREIFENKLAU: Johannes.

JOHANNES: And....

GREIFENKLAU: And?

JOHANNES: Examining Chief.

CARUSO: Further?

JOHANNES: And eh....

GREIFENKLAU: Speak out, man!

JOHANNES: Commander of the execution squad. But I was forced to do it. I did not do it out of my free will. I received orders. [*Points at* GREIFENKLAU.] It was he who said I should do it! [*Sobs.*] It is he who is to blame. Not me! Him!

CARUSO *gavels.*

GREIFENKLAU: The man has it completely right. I was his superior. He obeyed orders. Did his duty. He did what is, what always was, what always will be a soldier's first duty, to show blind obedience.

CARUSO: [*Stands up and goes down to the accused.*] My name is Caruso Gentile. Do either of the defendants recognize me?

GREIFENKLAU: [*Smiling.*] I have been the judge in several hundred cases. It is impossible that I can remember every single face. I don't know you.

CARUSO: Defendant Number 2 do you remember that you once had to administer disciplinary punishment before executing that same prisoner?

JOHANNES: Oh! He is dead! He was shot then! Herr Doctor! Herr Major! Herr General!

CARUSO: I was found alive after the attempted murder. [*The two defendants stare at him.*] Father Michelangelo is the witness.

PICCOLINO: He was found barely alive, suffering grievously from several gunshot wounds

GREIFENKLAU: You survived the fusillade?

CARUSO: Since the days of my ancestor the condottier Attila Gentile, my family has been famous for their exceptional thick skin. His grandson Eugenio Theodore Barba survived a strangulation.

GREIFENKLAU: [*Icily.*] Corporal Schulze. How does the execution resolution number 4 section 2 read?

JOHANNES: [*Snaps to attention, shouts.*] Yes sir, Herr General! "After the completion of the volley of the shooting, the commander of the squad shall inspect the executed and shall fire a security shot from his pistol to the back of the head of the executed."

GREIFENKLAU: Were the instructions followed?

JOHANNES: Herr Major, I …, I….

GREIFENKLAU: Sloppy. Complacent. Slipshod in the service. You are a person without a fatherland.

JOHANNES: Herr General.

GREIFENKLAU: Timeserver. [*Points to* CARUSO *and pronounces*] You see what can happen when one foresakes one's duty!

JOHANNES: I swear that I'll never forget again.

GREIFENKLAU: To think you are a teacher forming the souls of children!

JOHANNES: Can you not forgive... Lord God!

CARUSO: We resume the case.

GREIFENKLAU: I *object*!

CAVALLI: The case is open and shut. You participated in the murders here twenty years ago.

SANDRO: Guilty. You shall squirm.

FIDELE: Guilty!

PICCOLINO: Number 1 has objected. Let us listen.

CAVALLI: Guilty!

CARUSO: The court continues in session. Sssh!

GREIFENKLAU: I will enter my *objection*!

CARUSO: Against what?

GREIFENKLAU: The aggrieved party who sits and

judges his own case.

CAVALLI: The members in every case always represent an injured group. The aggrieved party always judges their own case.

CARUSO: Objection denied.

SANDRO: Benjamino was my nephew. These pigs killed him!

FIDELE: He was my cousin.

PICCOLINO: I was his uncle on the other side. All are related here.

GREIFENKLAU: The court's foreman was himself condemned to the Law's highest punishment!

FIDELE: And a little extra.

GREIFENKLAU: This is ridiculous. The judge is disqualified.

CARUSO: [*Ritualistic.*] The judge is more qualified than any other court. All here have a brother, friend, kin killed. They know best what it means for folk to be murdered by a military court. Concerning my own position I am the only qualified judge in the world. Only someone condemned to be shot to death knows what it is like. Objection denied. Cavalli?

CAVALLI: Guilty.

SANDRO: Guilty.

PICCOLINO: Guilty.

FIDELE: Guilty.

CARUSO: The court now moves to sentencing and we have only to choose between acquittal and....

JOHANNES: [*Sobs.*]

GREIFENKLAU: I object.

CARUSO: Against what?

GREIFENKLAU: The defendants have not been defended.

CAVALLI: He's right.

FIDELE: We forgot that.

CARUSO: Was I defended? Was Benjamino defended? Was

Janusz and Rosa defended.

PICCOLINO: He should be defended.

CARUSO: Were we defended?

GREIFENKLAU: Of course you had your defense lawyer. But Lieutanent Colonel Klinger from the Occupation Army invoked his right not to address the court.

MARCO: You must have a defending lawyer.

FIDELE: We forgot that.

SANDRO: You shall swing.

CAVALLI: Defense!

PICCOLINO: He's right. You must have a defense.

CARUSO: Who will defend you? [*Silence.*] No one? [*Silence.*] We cannot proceed.

SANDRO: So we can't hang them if they don't have a defender?

FIDELE: It's a big joke. If one doesn't have defenders one can't be hanged in any case. It doesn't look good to the world.

SANDRO: I have changed my mind. You should have a defender.

CARUSO: Who will defend you. Someone must announce themselves for the defense.

CAVALLI: Father Piccolino.

FIDELE: Piccolino.

CARUSO: Pater Piccolino is nominated. [*Gavels.* PICCOLINO *doesn't answer.*] Marco will replace him as juror. We choose him for the defense. Right?

EVERYONE: Yes, yes, yes.

CARUSO: [*Gavels.*] Do you accept the choice?

PICCOLINO: [*Stands up.*] Under protest. But I say that I will do my utmost as the defender. [*Changes places with* MARCO.] Now that I exchanges places the problem has changed. Until now Defendant's Number 1 was my nephew's and many other's murderer. From this moment he is a man facing death. The same fate applies to Defendant Number 2. Both the defendants, the Judge and his hangman have once been children. Both had mothers who sang to them in their cradles. I draw the court's attention to the rule that as ye judge so shall ye be judged.

Defendant Number 1 what is the highest moral?

GREIFENKLAU: To do your duty.

PICCOLINO: What is the soldier's duty?

GREIFENKLAU: To obey orders.

PICCOLINO: Always and under every circumstance?

GREIFENKLAU: Always and under every circumstance.

SANDRO: I won't listen to such clap trap.

PICCOLINO: Defendant Number 2 do you have the same opinion as Defendant Number 1?

JOHANNES: Yes.

PICCOLINO: Marco as a member of "43" have you sworn loyalty to Caruso as the group's Captain and cannot violate your oath to have....

FIDELE: You cannot compare!

SANDRO: No tricks here.

PICCOLINO: Do you have the duty to obey, Marco, or do you not?

CAVALLI: No comparison.

PICCOLINO: You all have the duty to obey but….

CARUSO: You of course have the duty to obey but….

FIDELE: Benjamino and Rosa and Caruso were good people who helped an unfortunate refugee from the camp. Janusz was a good person even though he cracked under questioning. They were abused and shot and they were good people. That can't be explained away.

MARCO: You are guilty of murder, both!

PICCOLINO: How many people did you shoot?

MARCO: 143.

PICCOLINO: You Caruso?

CARUSO: 182.

PICCOLINO: And all these people were evil?

CARUSO: They were soldiers and....

PICCOLINO: I asked if they were evil.

CARUSO: They were occupiers, they were!

SANDRO: We can't examine every case before hand.

MARCO: It would be a fine war if we should make such fine distinctions.

CARUSO: These two here are guilty.

FIDELE: They abused and killed people who were doing good. They are evil.

PICCOLINO: They are evil therefore they shall die?

THE COURT: Yes.

PICCOLINO: Why are they evil?

FIDELE: They have done evil.

PICCOLINO: All who have done evil, are evil. Is that so?

MARCO: Yes.

PICCOLINO: All who are evil, shall die?

SANDRO: Yes.

CARUSO: Demagogery! Objection!

PICCOLINO: Objection overruled. Defendant Number 1 where did you learn that the soldier's highest moral is to obey orders?

GREIFENKLAU: In my civic studies at the Military academy and from my father.

PICCOLINO: Where did your father learn it?

GREIFENKLAU: In his civic studies at the Military academy and from his father.

SANDRO: So they are all guilty.

PICCOLINO: Defendant Number 1, do you feel yourself guilty?

GREIFENKLAU: Guilty? Me?

PICCOLINO: Mea culpa, mea maxima culpa?

GREIFENKLAU: [*Turns around, singing.*]

"Mea Maxima Culpa"

I know not where I heard it last.
"Who is a human being and is not conscience striken?
Who is a human being who knows not
that he lives in dread of justice?"

This is my summation of all I have seen:
I hope God lets mercy substitute for justice.
I hope God in Heaven will say
Justice, children, that we can forget.

Ask me about "guilt." It is a cruel word.
Everything is to blame for all that happens on this earth.
In shame you can turn your face;
what one has sinned, we all have done.

We have seen innocence and have tarnished it.
Our own great guilt is all we have remaining.
We have seen dishonor and we let it happen
until dishonor is all we can see.

We have suffered injustice, we give it back in turn.
And we became murderers that same evening.
One acts blindly. One in best intentions
while one is red to one's elbows in blood!

Jens Bjørneboe

In our heart the law abides
and each jot of it stands with power.
All is as evil pictures from a drunk.
Of the earth we made a slaughter house.

Ach we must bow in shame and say:
Justice, God it frightens us.
Who is the man who does not know.
We need grace and the mercy of thy bosom!

I know not where I heard it last:
Who is a human being and not guilt ridden.

[*Turns quickly back to the court; Loudly:*] No my gentlemen. I do not feel myself to be guilty.

PICCOLINO: Defendant Number 2 where did you learn that the soldier's highest duty is to obey orders?

JOHANNES: In school, from my father, and in the army [*Points.*] from him.

PICCOLINO: The foreman of the Jury; in private life you are a mechanic. If a car kills someone will you then condemn and punish the car?

CARUSO: Man has free will. People are not cog wheels!

SANDRO: [*Screaming.*] Human beings are not machines.

Vehement uproar with shouts, screams, jumping around, blows and calls.

PICCOLINO: When I became an ordained priest, I promised obedience to my superior. My highest duty I must acknowledge is my obedience to the church. In its time of strength the church tried to force all heretics and dissidents to confess while being tortured and the guilty were burned alive at the stake. In all circumstances it was our duty to show obedience to our spiritual and worldly authorities. Otherwise we were punished.

CARUSO: Spoken like an anarchist!

MARCO: He's right. All authorities are evil. The church is evil and governments are evil.

PICCOLINO: The honor of the court. If the court condemns the defendant here then it must also condemn the defendant's ancestor, grandfather, father and teacher, superiors and government. The court must condemn all who stand behind them. They were employed for their activities and their payment was taken from taxes. All who pay taxes must hang. I demand a full acquittal on all charges for both defendants. They were only following their nature and upbringing to do their duty.

SANDRO: Guilty.

MARCO: Guilty.

FIDELE: Guilty.

CAVALLI: Guilty.

PICCOLINO: Human guilt is complicity in the evil. Is mankind all good or all evil? Cavalli, I ask you.

CAVALLI: Some are more good and some are more evil.

PICCOLINO: During the Franco Prussian war the Germans occupied France. Winter came and the Germans needed fuel. The French government was abroad in exile. In order to get wood the Germans told the French farmers that they should give wood to the Germans. Sabotage would be punished by death. On their side the French Government announced that all who did not sabotage the Germans would be punished by death. According to International Law both governments had jurisdiction. Who was unjust?

Silence.

Of course the civilians were outlaws. The French population were in either circumstance guilty.

Either in sabotage or in collaboration. Whatever one did one must be punished with death. For both sides are, according to International law, punishable. In a war the civilian population is always outlaw.

GREIFENKLAU: Holy Father, this analysis is completely correct.

PICCOLINO: And why?

CAVALLI: Governments have the weapons and they make the laws.

PICCOLINO: And a government always feels itself more colleaguial and more loyal to another government than to its own people. Does that mean that the civilian population is evil?

MARCO: On the contrary.

PICCOLINO: Formerly these two defendants were armed and you were civilians. Today it is these two who are civilians. Does that mean that you are evil?

MARCO: We won't allow ourselves to be tricked this way.

SANDRO: Read out the sentence, Caruso.

CARUSO: Both are to be hanged by the neck from the rope until dead.

PICCOLINO: Objection. The defense has not rested yet. The guilty are not the two men we have in front of us but their fathers, uncles, grandfathers, ancestors, their people and government. Who seduced them? Who had first said that the highest virtue is obedience to the authorities? When we have found the answers to that then we can ask who is really guilty.

FIDELE: These two shall hang. They are evil.

PICCOLINO: How are they evil? As their defender I raise the question: How did evil come into the world?

CARUSO: Execute the judgement now. Marco get to it. Fidele tie their hands together.

MARCO: Captain! [*To the defendants.*] Hands behind your backs!

FIDELE: [*Takes a long turn and approaches the two.*] Yes sir, Captain. [*The defendants are bound as* JOHANNES *cries.*]

PICCOLINO: As the defender I demand that I be allowed to continue my plea.

CARUSO: What does the Court say?

SANDRO: No.

CAVALLI: Five more minutes.

FIDELE: Yeah, yeah.

CARUSO: Granted; five minutes.

PICCOLINO: Caruso, my former student in Sunday School. [*The following proceeds like a cathecism in an abstract singing chant.*] How did evil come into the world? [*Question and response in ritual singing.*]

CARUSO: Cain struck Abel dead.

PICCOLINO: Wrong. Before that?

CARUSO: The snake tempted Eve with the apple and she disobeyed God and she bit it.

PICCOLINO: Wrong. How did the snake come into the world?

CARUSO: The highest of the Lord's angels, Lucifer, refused to serve God. He broke his obedience to the Lord.

The speech returns to ordinary rational prose.

PICCOLINO: Lucifer's highest virtue was obedience to God always and under every circumstance. Who was therefore the first to demand obedience to the authorities. [*Silence.*] Who was evil—God or Lucifer?

EVERYONE: [*Hooting and hollering*]

SANDRO: No one can say.

PICCOLINO: You don't even know how evil came into the world but to sit in judgment that you can do? And how has the world carried on the last 6,000 years? As the defender I request an answer to the question: What is the way of the world?

Both PICCOLINO *and the others switch over to a mass-like sing song in the question and answer.*

PICCOLINO: Cavalli what did the Romans do with the Christians?

CAVALLI: Burned them alive as torches.

PICCOLINO: What did the Christians do with the Jews? Fidele you had a Jewish father.

FIDELE: [*Sings*] For 2,000 years they have persecuted them. Whipped them to death, killed them with gas.

PICCOLINO: What has the Church done with the heretics? Marco, answer!

MARCO: Burnt them alive.

PICCOLINO: The Puritans and other persecuted ones who emigrated to America to find freedom. What did they do with the Negroes, Sandro?

SANDRO: Strung them up in the trees and burnt them alive.

PICCOLINO: What did the Turks do with the Armenians, Marco?

MARCO: Drove them out into the desert and let them die of thirst, the women, the children, and the old until all were dead.

PICCOLINO: Fidele I ask you; what did the English do with the Irish?

FIDELE: Shot them and hung them. Burned their towns.

PICCOLINO: What did the Japanese do with the prisoners during the war? Cavalli, what did they do?

CAVALLI: They tied them to the stakes and let them die of thirst.

PICCOLINO: What did the French do with the Algerians?

EVERYONE: [*Singing.*] Electrocution!

PICCOLINO: What did the Communists do when they got power?

EVERYONE: [*Shouting and screaming.*] Everyone knows that! [*Yelling and screaming.*] They built slave camps!

PICCOLINO: Marco, what did the Americans do with the Japanese?

Long pause.

MARCO: [*Singing.*]

"The Ballad of the City of Hiroshima"
Melody like a penny ballad.

The Bird Lovers

It was a beautiful morning,
in the city of Hiroshima.
A summer morning nineteen and forty-five.
And the sun shined bright,
from a sky without a cloud.
A summer morning nineteen and forty-five.

The little girls they played
by the sea and through the trees
and doing everything the grown-ups do.
They dressed their dolls
and they washed their doll clothes.
And the women sliced the bread on the kitchen
table.

And many little children there were
who were still lying in bed
for it was an early morning hour.
While the sun beamed lovely
and while the dew lay upon the meadow
and the flowers had just opened their petals.

It was a beautiful morning,
in the city of Hiroshima.
A summer morning nineteen and forty-five.
And the sun shined bright,
from a sky without a cloud.
A summer morning nineteen and forty-five.

PICCOLINO: [*Prose speak.*] Caruso what did the accused do to you?

CARUSO: They beat us with sticks and shot us against the wall.

PICCOLINO: And Sandro what will you do with them?

EVERYONE: [*Shouting.*] Justice. [*Pointing to the ropes.*]

PICCOLINO: Defendant Number 1 when did you become a bird lover?

GREIFENKLAU: [*Slowly and calmly.*] It was a long time ago. I don't remember.... It was while I was a boy. Maybe very early. I was immensely fond of birds early on. They were so innocent. It was while I walked to school. My father was an officer. My grandfather was also. On the way to school I saw several. I never was late for school. Never once. But one day I saw something under the eaves of the gable by the cellar window. It was a bird and a cat. I had to hurry so as not to be late. I was an obedient child. I ran as fast as I could the rest of the way to school. I believe it began then. Once I nursed a sick sparrow. I always loved small birds. I held him in my hands like so...the sparrow.

PICCOLINO: And the flowers?

GREIFENKLAU: Roses, especially roses.

PICCOLINO: Defendant Number 2, you are a bird lover. When did you become one?

JOHANNES: I don't know. Well during the war. I was very fond of small birds. There was so much that I had to do and so I became fond of small birds, especially song birds. I learned that from him. [*Nods towards* GREIFENKLAU.]

PICCOLINO: And flowers?

JOHANNES: Yes, yes flowers, roses. It was a hard war.

GREIFENKLAU *and* JOHANNES: [*Singing as an antiphony or canon*]

[*Duet*]

GREIFENKLAU:

Do you remember when fate brought us together?

JOHANNES:

In Nineteen and thirty-five.

GREIFENKLAU:

Do you remember how we shared all our labors

and board?

JOHANNES:

Until we eventually came home safe and sound.
Do you remember how we shared all our labors and board?

GREIFENKLAU:

Until we eventually came home safe and sound.

BOTH:

Do you remember when fate brought us together?
In Nineteen and thirty-five.
Do you remember how we shared all our labors and board?
Until we eventually came home safe and sound.

PICCOLINO: As the Defender I now close my case. I demand a new poll of the jury.

CARUSO: A new poll is agreed to. Sandro?

SANDRO: Guilty.

MARCO: Guilty.

FIDELE: Guilty.

CAVALLI: Guilty.

EVERYONE: [*Hollering, yelling, screaming.*] Guilty! Guilty! Guilty!

CARUSO: [*Standing.*] The Court finds....

[*All rising.*] Defendants 1 and 2 are found guilty by the court and are condemned to hang by the neck from the rope until dead. Sandro, Cavalli, Fidele, Marco!

They place the defendants on the plank straddling the two boxes and put the ropes around their necks. JOHANNES *resists and cries.*

CARUSO: Those who were judged are now the executioners. We'll kick the boxes away together! One! Two!!

PICCOLINO: Wait...as priest I have the last word! *As the priest*!

CARUSO: Okay but make it short. We got to get up early tomorrow.

PICCOLINO: Economics is our town's weakness. The travel resort has a planned capacity of 20,000 guests per year. Of the Bird Friends over half will be women. That means at least 10 to 15,000 hairdressings through the year, some part of which will be permanents. The chances for a capable hair dresser will be enormous. That means opportunities....

CAVALLI: [*Shouting.*] That's what I've been saying the whole time!

PICCOLINO: Caruso, I have instructed your son Andrea at school. He is a handy boy who could well run a big mechanical workshop. The Bird Lovers come from a country that has the most motorized vehicles per capita of all the countries in the world. Do you have the right to destroy his future? You can expand and build a real service station in Torre Rosse.

CARUSO: They shall hang! Mercenaries!

PICCOLINO: Just because many will have cars doesn't mean everyone will have one. The need for cabs and other means of transportation that can bring the visitors out to our natural surroundings will be immense. Marco if I were you, I would invest in getting at least two cars for that purpose. Preferably more. Your son, whom I have taught for several years, is one of those young men who really merits higher training. Between you and me, one can say, he is a gifted young man. He can go a long way if he gets a good start. Do you want him to become a lawyer or a doctor?

MARCO: I have been thinking of that all along. Cavalli I stand entirely on your side!

CAVALLI: We stand together.

PICCOLINO: A great part of the Bird Lovers are indeed vegetarians, Fidele, but that doesn't mean that they never need prepared food. I don't need to spell out what this means for everyone in the restaurant business. The Bird Friends love potatoes and cabbage together with their food stuffs. In several years you will have a big restaurant here. Your three daughters can have the dowries they deserve and....

FIDELE: I was the first to mention that!

CAVALLI: I was the very first one!

CARUSO: I urge you. Don't let yourself be bought!

MARCO: It's Christian to show mercy. [*They bellow and stomp.*]

SANDRO: It's too late. They are condemned to death and they will dangle. [*Wants to push the boxes away.*] You know they are guilty! We have condemned them! [*The others hold him back.*]...to death!

CAVALLI: We can pardon them. It is a simple case.

SANDRO: No, no, no. Hang they must!

FIDELE: This is pure and shameless self-concern. It is because he is not going to get something for himself. He is in agriculture!

SANDRO: A farm worker never gets a good deal. Even if the town becomes filthy rich I will still get the same miserable hourly pay. They *shall* hang. [*Silence.*]

CARUSO: You must understand that it is too late to pardon them. They will report us and will relocate their travel resort to another place, afterwards. [*Pause, uncertainty.*]

PICCOLINO: If I have not misjudged Number 1 regards his word just as high as his unquestioning obedience to his general staff and his government, irregardless of the government he works for. [*Pause.*]

GREIFENKLAU: You have my word of honor as an *officer*.

CARUSO: An officer and a policeman gets paid to do everything that is required of him without having any opinions himself. An officer is a whore!

He is paid to be obedient!

SANDRO: You shall dangle.

MARCO: We will really see what we can do for you, Sandro. It would be wrong if you must continue as before without getting your share of the prosperity, only the old hourly pittance. You must take part in our progress!

FIDELE: You can join me, as a waiter.

CAVALLI: Naturally we will help you…and….

MARCO: You can be your own man, you too. We will help you to get your own land, so you can sell cabbage and tomatoes to the vegetarians who will come here to hear the birds sing and….

CARUSO: You're lying! Don't listen to them.

SANDRO: I can't trust you. You never helped me before.

CAVALLI: We never had the opportunity to do so, before.

FIDELE: Now there will be opportunities if only the Bird Lovers come and everyone gets rich.

MARCO: You can really be one of us, Sandro, when the money comes.

CARUSO: When, when, when! We know what we got. The two murderers there. But we don't know what we will get. Sandro you're on my side.

CAVALLI: The murderers are not really that bad. When everything is said and done they have only been found guilty of having taken a salary to do dirty work. They are like the garbage collector except they are not as useful.... We promise that we will help you, Sandro. Only we got to get started ourselves.

CARUSO: Sandro!

FIDELE: We can help him with guarantees. That's how he can take over the farm after old Giovanni....

CAVALLI: Write it down. I'll get in on it also.

CARUSO: Sandro, listen.

MARCO: If you can guarantee it Father Piccolino. I am willing with what little I have to....

PICCOLINO: Never under Heaven will my signature have any worth. If you three sign it that will be good enough.

FIDELE: So you will be one of us, Sandro.

CARUSO: No. You are not one of them. You are a farm worker.

SANDRO: I would rather be a landowner.

CAVALLI: That you will be.

CARUSO: You are betraying me?

SANDRO: So I can get someone to work for me.

FIDELE: All you need to do is to count your profits.

PICCOLINO: One can well anticipate the Bird Friends will guarantee the sale of your product, for example, of salad, cauliflower and what have you. Whatever. Some rather big contracts I should think. For a good price....

CARUSO: Don't sell yourself, Sandro. They are deceiving you.

PICCOLINO: Both men and produce have their price and their moment.

CAVALLI: We have promised that. Now you'll get enough to get married.

SANDRO: [*Brooding.*] If I marry, can I save enough to set up a household?

PICCOLINO: What is your position, defendant Number 1? Can the management of the travel resort make a long term commitment?

GREIFENKLAU: We could probably commit ourselves to buy his products with naturally certain specifications and in legal business form at a price higher than the customary wholesale rates and also under market prices of course with an index related to price developments on the open market if fruits and vegetables show a great fluctuation after a year's time, with rainfall and similar factors. Nothing shall hinder an agreement that is advantageous for both parties.

CAVALLI: It is to be regarded as a promised commitment given in full freedom and witnessed to.

GREIFENKLAU: I certainly feel myself freer if you will have the goodness to unbind me from this here. [*Indicates the rope around his neck and hands.*].... I mean naturally *us*. I could in full freedom and without coercion declare so in a written statement that will be binding both morally and judicially. Moreover I give my word.

CARUSO: I object.

SANDRO: Now I'll get my own house.

CARUSO: Don't touch them!

FIDELE: We naturally follow the democratic method. Those who can pay, choose.

CARUSO: They are murderers.

CAVALLI: Were.

SANDRO: Can't we have a written surety for this?

PICCOLINO: Of course. That can be done, Cavalli?

CAVALLI: Certainly, if he wants it.

CARUSO: These murderers have killed and tortured us.

CAVALLI: Not me.

CARUSO: Benjamino. Little Benjamino, they killed him like a dog and his Pole. They killed two innocents. [*Points.*] He burned out Janusz' eyes to get him to inform on us. Then he shot him.

MARCO: Not me.

SANDRO: Not me either.

CARUSO: Certainly *me*!

MARCO: This was a long time ago.

FIDELE: A real long time ago.

CARUSO: Have you really forgotten everything. Benjamino! Rosa! Janusz! Me! Have you forgotten that country town south of here? Where they burnt all the inhabitants inside the church. [*Quiet.*] They beat me, condemned me to death, set me up against the wall and shot me, and Janusz and Benjamino! You would do business with them!

SANDRO: You're only thinking about yourself.

CAVALLI: You're a real egotist, Caruso.

FIDELE: He lives in the past. It's sad that he's outlived his time.

CARUSO: I was scorned, tormented and executed. You

do business.

MARCO: Now that Sandro is getting his house and land.

SANDRO: And farm workers and wife and livestock.

PICCOLINO: Fidele all of you make a bond so the matter is settled.

FIDELE: Fine, fine....

CAVALLI: The children will receive an education. Come on. [*They free the prisoners.*]

CARUSO: [*Screaming.*] It was *them* we died for!

CAVALLI: Now we owe it to them to live.

GREIFENKLAU: [*Rubbing his hands.*] Do the gentlemen have a typewriter here or should I write it by hand? It's better with a typewriter and a couple of carbons so as to be as businesslike as possible. The greatest advantage for both parties. Two copies.

FIDELE: I have a typewriter in here.... [*Exits.*]

CARUSO: [*To* PICCOLINO.] Why do you do this to me?

FIDELE: [*Returns with a typewriter.*] Here! Blue paper and carbons. [*Sets the typewriter up.*] We'll bind the guarantees in a folder afterwards.

CAVALLI: Usual guarantees up to 30,000. It expands. Naturally with stipulations that the money is only drawn on secured properties.

GREIFENKLAU: [*Begin to type.*] We must naturally stipulate that the goods are of the standard market quality and in the quantities we need and with favorable terms of payment.

CARUSO: I can't watch this. [*Screams.*] Father forgive them not, for they *know* what they do!

CAVALLI: Don't bother us, be quiet. This is important.

GREIFENKLAU: [*Reading mechanically what he has typed.*] Therefore...undersigned state Advocate doctor juris Huldreich von und zu Greifenklau residing in Schweinsruhe, declares herewith on behalf of the Bird Lover's Group division of the National Society for Animal's.... [*Writes some more in silence. All watch him.*]

CARUSO: Has everyone forsaken me?

PICCOLINO: The Son of Man does not have a stone

where he can rest his head.

CARUSO: Do you love me?

PICCOLINO: I cherish you.

CARUSO: Piccolino you don't love me.

PICCOLINO: The world is governed by typewriters, police and money. But the greatest of the three is money. He who has money also has the police. Money moves mountains.

CARUSO: I can't live in such a world.

FIDELE: It's your only choice.

Pause. Everyone around the typewriter. GREIFENKLAU *writes.*

CARUSO: No! There is no need to go on.

Silence. He screams in a rage and goes to the rope. Everyone turns to watch him.

CAVALLI: Is it necessary to go on like that? We voted.

Everyone stares at CARUSO *for a moment then they turn to the typewriter.* GREIFENKLAU *types. Music from "The Death Song."*

CARUSO: [*Gets up on the box and sticks his head into the noose.*] Lord if thou art willing, remove this cup from me!

PICCOLINO: [*Looks at him and makes the sign of the cross.*]

MARCO: [*Sees* PICCOLINO.] What?

PICCOLINO: Peace be with him.

Everyone rises in silence and watches CARUSO.

CARUSO: It is better that a one man die for the people than that all the people be ruined.

SANDRO: This is strange....

FIDELE: Will he really....

PICCOLINO: A man has a fleeting time on the earth and his days are numbered.

CARUSO: For a second time I die for thine sake.

GREIFENKLAU: [*Slowly.*] Remarkable. What do you say, Johannes?

JOHANNES: It is as if this has a higher meaning. He received a death sentence twenty years ago and only now is it being fulfilled.

Long pause.

MARCO: It is practically the same death.

FIDELE: In reality he has been dead since that time.

CARUSO: [*Sings with a very strong voice.*]

"The Death Song"

Now the day has arrived and the hour has arrived.
And you are placed against the wall to bleed.
And the ones who hold you dear
Soon fade away from you
That's when you will see; it is lonesome to die.

Before the day has arrived and the hour has arrived.
And the sand you stand on, you have colored red.
When they are taking you to the other side
you'll remember what I said,
Brother it is really lonesome to be dead....

CARUSO *remains still with the noose around his neck. All wait in silence.*

SANDRO: Will he not....

FIDELE: Sssh. He's only thinking a little. Taking leave of and such....

Long pause.

SANDRO: I always think of messing around with fat women when someone is about to squirm.

EVERYONE: Sssh.

A very long pause.

CARUSO: [*Screams.*] I can't! [*Pulls his head out of the noose.*] I dare not! [*Pause.*]

CAVALLI: Now you are one of us.

EVERYONE: Yes, yes.

CARUSO: Yes.

FIDELE: You will join the Bird Friends.

CARUSO: Yes.

EVERYONE: To the Bird Friends. [*Music.*]

CAVALLI: Group "43" as a block passeth to the Bird Lovers.

CARUSO: [*Climbs down. The locals embrace him.*] There remains one more thing. [*Goes to the* JUDGE, *kneels.*] You condemned me to death.

GREIFENKLAU: Yes sir.

CARUSO: Can you pardon me?

GREIFENKLAU: [*Embraces him.*] Yes.

CARUSO: [*On all four to* JOHANNES.] You whipped me and shot me.

JOHANNES: Yes.

CARUSO: [*Bows his head, kneeling.*] Can you pardon me?

The Occupying Power's old emblem sinks down and fills the background.

JOHANNES: [*Bows down and lifts him up. Embraces him and kisses him.*]

The motif from the Ninth Symphony of Beethoven plays; "Seid umschlungen, Millionen!."

Jens Bjørneboe

Born in 1920, the Norwegian author Jens Bjørneboe was one of the most controversial authors of his day; highly outspoken, anarchic even, he fought with most social institutions in his determination to challenge censorship, repression, and authoritarianism. Novelist, poet, playwright, journalist and essayist, Bjørneboe published numerous works from the 1950s to his death in 1976.

Son of a shipowner and consul, Ingvald Bjønebo [sic] and Maja Svenson, the young Jens reacted to the provincialism of his home town by being expelled from several schools and running away to sea at the age of 16. He returned in 1939 for his father's death, and spent the years of the German occupation in Sweden.

His first artistic ambitions were directed at painting, but after the war he began to write, conducting his literary life as a series of campaigns which left behind a trail of court cases, outraged authorities, and scandals. Like his heroes, Bjørneboe modeled his life as a misfit, a deviant personality who insisted upon his "differences."

From adolescence on, Bjørneboe had been aware of the German atrocities, and after the war he felt compelled to investigate further the topic in his novel *Før hanen galer* (Before a Cock Crows, 1952). He continued to explore the terrifying paradoxes of behavior revealed by the Nazis, who murdered and experimented on Jews by day and returned to being loving husbands and fathers by night, in *Under en hårdere himmel* (Beneath a Harsher Sky, 1957); and in his fiction Bjørneboe also violently denounced the Norwegian persecution of Nazi sympathizers after the war. Teaching at the Steiner school in Oslo, a school that followed the educational theories of Rudolf Steiner, Bjørneboe turned his attacks to education, particularly in *Jonas* (1955).

In the late 1950s he traveled and lived for a while in Southern Europe, returning to Norway in 1960, where he remained to the end of his life. His attacks on authoritarian systems, however, saw no abatement. He attacked the penal system in *Din onde hyrde* (The Bad Shepherd, 1960), the judicial system in *Tilfellet Torgersen* (The Torgersen Case, 1973), and sexual mores in *Uten en tråd* (Without a Stitch, 1966). *Uten en tråd* was deemed pornography, and resulted in a trial in Norway in 1967.

During this same period Bjørneboe began to write for the stage, and emerged as Norway's most innovative playwright. Among his several plays are *Til lykke med dagen* (Congratulations, 1965), *Fugleelskerne* (translated in this volume) in 1966, and *Amputasjon* (Amputation, 1970).

In the early 1970s Bjørneboe returned to fiction, particularly in the trilogy *Frihetens øyeblikk* (Moment of Freedom), *Kruttårnet* (The Powder Magazine), and *Sillheten* (The Silence), produced between 1969 and 1973. These works, which he described as "The History of Bestiality," sought out to explore unanswerable questions of evil and guilt in the twentieth century. He continued this exploration in the adventure tale, *Haiene* (1974), translated recently as *The Sharks.* But the search to understand evil took a great emotional toll on him; an alcoholic and depressed, he committed suicide in 1976 at the age of 56.

Books in the Sun & Moon Classics

1 Gertrude Stein *Mrs. Reynolds*
2 Djuna Barnes *Smoke and Other Early Stories*
3 Stijn Streuvels *The Flaxfield**
4 Marianne Hauser *Prince Ishmael*
5 Djuna Barnes *New York*
6 Arthur Schnitzler *Dream Story*
7 Susan Howe *The Europe of Trusts*
8 Gertrude Stein *Tender Buttons*
9 Arkadii Dragomoschenko *Description**
10 David Antin *Selected Poems: 1963-1973**
11 Lyn Hejinian *My Life***
12 F. T. Marinetti *Let's Murder the Moonshine: Selected Writings*
13 Heimito von Doderer *The Demons*
14 Charles Bernstein *Rough Trades**
15 Fanny Howe *The Deep North**
16 Tarjei Vesaas *The Ice Palace*
17 Jackson Mac Low *Pieces O' Six**
18 Steve Katz *43 Fictions**
19 Valery Larbaud *Childish Things**
20 Wendy Walker *The Secret Service**
21 Lyn Hejinian *The Cell**
22 Len Jenkin *Dark Ride and Other Plays**
23 Tom Raworth *Eternal Sections**
24 Ray DiPalma *Numbers and Tempers: Selected Poems**
25 Italo Svevo *As a Man Grows Older*
26 André Breton *Earthlight**
27 Fanny Howe *Saving History**
28 F. T. Marinetti *The Untameables*
29 Arkadii Dragomoschenko *Xenia**
30 Barbara Guest *Defensive Rapture**
31 Carl Van Vechten *Parties*
32 David Bromige *The Harbormaster of Hong Kong**

33 Keith Waldrop *Light While There is Light: An American History**

34 Clark Coolidge *The Rova Improvisations**

35 Dominique Fourcade *Xbo**

36 Marianne Hauser *Me & My Mom**

37 Arthur Schnitzler *Lieutenant Gustl*

38 Wilhelm Jensen/Sigmund Freud *Gradiva/Delusion and Dream in Gradiva*

39 Clark Coolidge *Own Face*

40 Susana Thénon *distancias/distances**

41 José Emilio Pacheco *A Distant Death**

42 Lyn Hejinian *The Cold of Poetry***

43 Jens Bjørneboe *The Bird Lovers**

44 Gertrude Stein *Stanzas in Meditation*

45 Jerome Rothenberg *Gematria**

46 Leslie Scalapino *Defoe**

47 Douglas Messerli, ed. *From the Other Side of the Century: A New American Poetry 1960–1990*

48 Charles Bernstein *Dark City**

49 Charles Bernstein *Content's Dream: Essays 1975–1984*

*First American publication

**Revised edition

THE BIRD LOVERS

JENS BJØRNEBOE

Translated from the Norwegian, with an Introduction by Frederick Wasser

A German delegation of bird lovers has descended upon a small Italian village in order to establish a bird sanctuary. The local "hunting club" not only claims war on the delegates because of their love of eating nightingales and larks, but because—made up as they are of former Italian partisans—they recognize in the bird lovers two former Nazi executioners. Carefully they plot to capture the former Nazis and bring them to trial.

But the kangaroo trial which takes up the second act of this engrossing and forceful study of evil ends in an unexpected manner, as the so-called judges are forced to study the nature of evil—and the nature of themselves.

Jens Bjørneboe's tragic-comic work, first produced as "Fugleelskerne" in Oslo, Norway in 1966, is a paradoxical morality play in which easy answers to the nature of power, love, and evil are shown up as these very forces themselves.

Author of the noted novels *Moment of Freedom* and *The Sharks,* and of numerous other works, Bjørneboe died in Norway in 1976.

$9.95